Resisting *Brown*

Composition, Literacy, and Culture
David Bartholomae and Jean Ferguson Carr, Editors

Resisting *Brown*

Race, Literacy, and Citizenship in the Heart of Virginia

Candace Epps-Robertson

University of Pittsburgh Press

Published by the University of Pittsburgh Press, Pittsburgh, Pa., 15260
Copyright © 2018, University of Pittsburgh Press
Manufactured in the United States of America
Printed on acid-free paper
10 9 8 7 6 5 4 3 2 1

Cataloging-in-Publication data is available from the Library of Congress

ISBN 13: 978-0-8229-6555-8
ISBN 10: 0-8229-6555-0

Cover art: Protesters on Main Street, Farmville, Virginia, July 1963, #015. Farmville 1963 Civil Rights Protests, Virginia Commonwealth University James Branch Cabell Library. Special Collections and Archives.
Cover design: Joel W. Coggins

To my grandmother, Kathryn Wright Anderson. Her patience, love, and dreams continue to carry me farther than I ever believed I would go.

Contents

Acknowledgments

My earliest memories are of playing school at my grandma's house. This was long before I'd even set foot in a *real* classroom. Even though she called it "play-school," it was quite real. There was a school desk we'd move into the living room, as well as a pale green lunch tray I used to go through the mock lunch line she set up in the kitchen, and the backyard was complete with a swing and seesaw my grandpa built from leftover wood he'd haul. I had a chalkboard and loads of books, paper, and pens. My grandma taught me how to read. I can't remember that first book I read, but I remember her hand covering mine as she moved my finger across the page, touching each letter as we read aloud together. I could not have imagined then that I would ever write a book of my own, and I am grateful for the support I have received from so many to allow this project to come to fruition.

This project originally began at Syracuse University in the Composition and Cultural Rhetoric Program. I had the good fortune of forming relationships with scholars who are both brilliant and thoughtful. Patient, thorough, and kind, Dr. Lois Agnew has provided me with unyielding support both during my time at Syracuse and beyond. Drs. Gwendolyn Pough, Eileen Schell, Adam Banks, Steve Parks, and Iswari Pandey provided critical feedback when the project was in its earliest stages. I also thank Dr. Louise Wetherbee Phelps, whose mentoring has been critical to my development as a scholar balancing commitments to work and home. Additionally, I have a network of colleagues and friends who have been more than generous with their time and support. Brian Baille, April Baker-Bell, Stuart Blythe, Tamika Carey, Mary Chapman Cook, Laura Davies, Terese Guinsatao Monberg, Bump Halbritter, Bill Hart-Davidson, Krista Kennedy, Julie Lindquist, Edward Peeples, Malea Powell, Justin Reid, Tricia Serviss, Sara Webb-Sunderhaus, and Lacy Ward, I thank each of you for the conversations, reassurance, and support.

I could not have completed this manuscript without institutional support. During my time at Michigan State University (MSU), support from my chair, Dr. Jeff Grabill, provided me with a nurturing and creative work environment. Additionally, a grant from the MSU Humanities and Arts Research Program allowed me a semester of research leave. My colleagues at Old Dominion University were kind and gracious. A course release at Old Dominion University allowed me to finalize research for the book. Finally, support from my department and colleagues at the University of North Carolina helped to finalize this project.

I am also grateful for Josh Shanholtzer, Alex Wolfe, and the many others from the University of Pittsburgh Press. My reviewers provided thoughtful comments and feedback. I am grateful for their time.

A project such as this can't exist without the help of archives and archivists. This project would not have been possible without the support of former Virginia State University Special Collections archivist Luscious Edwards. His knowledge of Virginia history and the African American civil rights movement was invaluable. I am appreciative of the assistance I received at the Library of Virginia and the University of Virginia's Albert and Shirley Small Special Collections Library.

This project could not have been completed without my family. My grandmother first shared her stories with me about Prince Edward County. She also taught me how to listen and dream. Both actions are necessary to survive and thrive in the academy. My mother, Iris Epps, was one of the first in our family to go to college. She set the bar high with her intelligence, work ethic, and kindness. The first person to ever teach me the importance of arguing effectively was my father, LaRue DuFay Epps. He also gave me the mantra that helped me get through the process of writing a book: "It can be done." The unwavering support of my brother, David Epps, often came in the form of late-night conversations that involved donuts or music. I am grateful that he knows how to get me out of my own head. My mother-in-law, Peggy Robertson, is a fountain of knowledge when it comes to Virginia history. My husband, Hunter Robertson, has made more sacrifices than I can count so that I could complete this project. His commitment to our family is a gift. My daughters, Phoenix and Artemis, are a constant source of motivation. Their curiosity, refusal to settle for simple answers, and love of play are constant sources of inspiration for me. I am grateful that they don't mind having a mom who writes a book during car line and ukulele practice.

I am indebted to those from Prince Edward County who were willing to share their time and stories with me. I am grateful for the learning experiences I had with Rev. Everett Berryman, Alijah "Mickie" Pride, Armstead "Chuckie" Reid, Shirley Earley, Clara Johnson, and Bernetta Watkins. The Robert Russa Moton Museum in Farmville, Virginia, is dedicated to telling the story of the five-year public schools closure. The museum, once the site of the county's all Black high school, also served as the Free School's high school building. It has been a place for learning and healing in the community, and I am thankful for the space they provided for me to do many of these interviews.

Portions of chapter 2 appeared in "The Race to Erase *Brown v. Board of Education*: The Virginia Way and the Rhetoric of Massive Resistance," published in *Rhetoric Review*, vol. 35, no. 2, 2016, pp. 108–20. It is reprinted with permission.

Preface

A Genealogy through Stories

From the earliest rocking of my cradle, I had known about the capers Brer
Rabbit is apt to cut and what the Squinch Owl says from the house top. But it
was fitting me like a tight chemise. I couldn't see it for wearing it. It was only
when I was off in college, away from my native surroundings, that I could see
myself like somebody else and look at my garment.

Zora Neale Hurston, *Folklore, Memoirs, and Other Writings*

Resisting Brown: Race, Literacy, and Citizenship in the Heart of Virginia presents
the history of a small Virginia county's resistance to *Brown v. Board of Education*
by those in power and the role of literacy and citizenship training in countering
that resistance. Prince Edward County, just sixty miles south of the erstwhile
capital of the Confederacy, Richmond, stands as a microcosm of America's struggles with race, education, and citizenship after *Brown*. The county's board of supervisors, unwilling to implement integration after the *Brown* decision, took the
drastic measure of closing all public schools in May 1959. Those schools would
remain closed for the next five years. The rationale for the closures, which were
an explicit act of defiance against *Brown*, was entrenched in racialized constructions of citizenship and ideologies that maintained white control over Black lives
through sanctioned segregation. The Black community and its allies made numerous resistance efforts during the five-year closure period, among them the
Prince Edward County Free School Association.[1] The Free School, the only formal, free K–12 education available in the county during the closures, opened on
September 16, 1963. This temporary school system served approximately 1,567
students, both Black and white, aged six through twenty-three.

The Free School offered students a complete K–12 experience, with courses
in math, reading, social studies, and science, as well as extracurricular activities. The curriculum, however, placed special emphasis on reading, writing, and
speaking as skills necessary for fulfilling the roles of engaged citizens. The Free
School utilized pedagogical practices and curricula that were at the forefront

of educational research for the time period. The teachers, students, faculty, and parents collaborated to support the needs of a most unique community. The Free School's philosophy statement presented its commitment to both students and a community that reached far beyond the walls of the school: "Literacy presumes more than the teaching of the '3 R's.' It presumes training to think and observe carefully, and the effort to formulate answers that are important to our civilization. Content must influence students to think clearly, so as to be able to sift the truths from the untruths when scrutinizing our democratic processes as well as the governmental processes of other world peoples" (Sullivan, "Prince Edward County Free School Association" [Handbook]). Thus, the teaching of literacy practices was connected to a desire to have students learn how to think critically and globally about democratic processes. Given the circumstances of Prince Edward County in 1963, the mission met the challenge.

School administrators and teachers encouraged literacy as key to democratic engagement and required students to practice literacy both inside and outside of the classroom in myriad ways. The school itself was an argument against segregationists' claims about what Blacks and whites could and could not do together, as well as the authorities' incessantly expressed stereotypes about the Black community's educational needs. The Free School's explicit response to segregationists' constructions of citizenship and withholding of public education was manifested in the school's mission statement, philosophy, and curricular guides and demonstrated through the pedagogical commitments of teachers. My analysis of the Free School illustrates how this institution challenged white articulations of citizenship that sought to control the Black community. The Free School presented students with opportunities to gain the skills and experiences necessary to advance engaged citizenship and recognized the knowledge and expressions of citizenship students brought with them. In its commitment to preparing students to be democratic participants, a commitment that ultimately mirrored what public schools had historically been designed to offer, the Free School figured literacy as a direct response. The events that transpired in Prince Edward County are horrendous examples of the possibilities of white supremacist ideology. As this book shows, the Free School's response is evidence of the ingenuity required in crafting institutional and community-driven responses to counter the insidiousness of structural racism.

My introduction to the Free School came first from my grandmother, Kathryn Wright Anderson. She grew up in Prince Edward County, spending her first seventeen years in Farmville, a small town that is the county seat of Prince Edward. My grandmother married and left the county in 1947, but many of her nieces, nephews, and other relatives suffered the loss of opportunity from the school closures. Some family members speak freely about their experiences, while others choose not to share stories. I never witnessed the closures or experienced them directly; the experiences of my family members are with me through both the silences and the stories. I share my family's history because this positionality matters.

Where I'm from in the South, you often start introductions with a genealogy. Depending on the setting and audience, this could be as simple as naming your hometown or as detailed as listing great-great-grandparents, second cousins, and when and where your parents met. In academia, we do something similar when we chronicle where we received our degrees and name our mentors. In both contexts, we describe these chains because they matter. For some, our family and academic lineages tell others about our histories, our geographies, and our commitments. This book is an expression of my academic commitments to contribute to our field's efforts at understanding historical connections among race, rhetoric, literacy, and citizenship, but I would be remiss if I did not describe the role of my grandmother's stories.

My grandmother, like scholars of rhetoric and literacy studies, knew that stories were not just talk. For her, stories were a tapestry of lessons and histories, and often a catalyst for action. She practiced what we theorize and describe as the importance of storytelling. Stories have the ability to incite paradigm shifts in our collective histories. Scholars in rhetoric and composition continue to recount the significance of stories as practice for understanding histories of rhetoric (King, Gubele, and Anderson; Powell). I fondly remember many of the stories my grandmother told me about growing up in Prince Edward County, but there were dark stories, too. She told me about her first job as a domestic, when she was only nine. She told me that to buy shoes in downtown Farmville, Black people had to trace their feet on a sheet of paper, because store owners wouldn't let them try on shoes. She described young Black boys being displayed in the storefront of the candy shop as spectacles of entertainment on Main Street, eating peanuts for the amusement of white observers. Her stories most often ended with a sigh and reminder of how different things were for me.

I recall that her first time telling me about the schools closing frightened me. I was about six or seven, sitting at her kitchen table and coloring while she was standing over the stove preparing supper. I don't quite recall how the subject came up, but she was moving quickly from the stovetop to the counter, cutting potatoes and sifting salt into the boiling water for beef hash. I listened intently, as always, to every word she said. She began her story slowly: "There were laws to keep us out of places, but sometimes there wasn't even a law, it was just what you knew." I didn't grasp the threat she implied, but I recognized a catch in her voice I had only ever heard when she talked about the death of her own mother.

She stopped her rhythm of cutting, sifting, and stirring, turned toward me at the table, and said with emphasis, "Most of the time, white folks didn't want us anywhere 'round them. We cooked and cleaned for them, but you had to be invisible about it. Child, they didn't want us in their schools. They wanted to keep us separate so bad they closed down all the schools, put chains on the doors, and said, 'We don't want no niggras in here.'" She wiped her face and moved back to her post at the stove. She didn't speak any more about it that day, but we'd return to this story and others throughout my childhood. Her emotion never waned over the years when she spoke about the racism she encountered. Her wounds were still raw, and she often encouraged me to push beyond the Mason Dixon line.

As I got older I learned that many of the experiences my grandmother described were common across the South and not unheard of in the North. What separates Prince Edward County from other localities, however, is the five-year absence of public education for both Black and white students. Resistance to *Brown* was common, but in Prince Edward it was extreme. Massive Resistance, as segregationists termed their response to *Brown*, took many forms. One hundred and one members of Congress from the South signed the Southern Manifesto in February 1956, vowing to resist integration. Many localities across the South instituted policies aimed at thwarting *Brown*. As a state, Virginia led the Massive Resistance movement with a legislative package aimed at inhibiting integration, with allowances that ranged from permitting the governor to close any school that integrated to distributing tuition grants for white families who chose to send their children to private schools. The primary rationale behind these actions hinged on a logic that had existed in the South since the Civil War: white southerners knew best what both Black and white communities needed.

While the stories of Prince Edward's resistance are histories I grew up with, the county's resistance is not often included as part of the larger narrative we hear about the civil rights movement's pursuit of equitable education. Christopher Bonastia's *Southern Stalemate: Five Years without Public Education in Prince Edward County, Virginia*, posits that attention to Prince Edward County's role at the forefront of Virginia's resistance has been scant because it lacked the kind of drama that marked other sites during the civil rights movement (11). Violence was rare and locked-out children suffered quietly, without hoses and dogs turned on them. Prince Edward County's story may not have garnered the same attention as other sites, but for those committed to understanding how resistance is both employed and countered, how citizenship is constructed and practiced, and the roles of rhetoric and literacy in these moments, Prince Edward County's drastic anti-integration measure presents a significant case.

In this book, I have three main goals. First, by examining the Free School, I seek to recover a history that often stands in the shadows of the American civil rights movement. Second, I hope to further our understanding of the historical connections between literacy and citizenship at a moment when citizenship was, as the political theorist Danielle Allen describes, being "reconstituted." Allen writes, "If we are to understand the nature of citizenship since 1957, and its requirements, we need to analyze the moment of desegregation, when the polity was coming unstitched and being rewoven" (4). The *Brown v. Board of Education* rulings (1954, 1955) redefined notions of public education and citizenship, and the Free School demonstrates a crucial response. Third, the Free School literacy curriculum and pedagogical practices provide contemporary teachers and scholars with a rich model of the possibilities (and perils) of what literacy programs designed to place citizenship at the forefront can be, as well as the importance of developing organic pedagogical practices to support students and their communities in these missions. I present the Free School as a unique institutional rhetoric that responded to multiple audiences' conceptions of citizenship, how it is taught, and its connection to literacy.

Like Zora Neale Hurston in the quote that opens this preface, I needed time and distance before I could come back to Prince Edward and see it as a place where I could begin to address some of the larger issues that concern me as a scholar. I originally came to this project in graduate school at a time when I was trying to figure out both who I was as a woman of color in the ivory tower and how I might take up projects that both honor the epistemologies outside of academia that nurtured me, along with the new ways of thinking and doing I was being introduced to. The more I investigated and encountered work from other scholars who were committed to understanding rhetorics and histories of race, rhetoric, and literacy, the more I could see the need to return to my own backyard.

This project is an expression of my commitment to honor the epistemologies of home within myself and those I encounter. I present this book in my role as both a scholar of rhetoric and literacy studies and as a granddaughter who once sat at the kitchen table and listened with love.

Resisting *Brown*

Introduction

The Power, Possibility, and Peril in Histories of Literacy

The history of the US public education system is the story of a nation that has continuously struggled to decide who gets educated and what type of education students should receive. While education was originally a privilege reserved for the rich, during the nineteenth century education reformers such as Horace Mann and Henry Barnard championed democratization through education. Mann saw mass education as a means to assist immigrants in becoming American and as a way to lessen the widening gap between the rich and the poor. The concept and practice of public education evolved alongside economic, political, and social upheavals the Civil War had brought on. The nation's landscape was changing, and the common school became the primary source of instruction for patriotism and civic values. In spite of hopes that free schooling could create a unified society, those in positions of power within the public education system and reformers working outside of institutional structures were not always able to articulate who public education would benefit. Diane Ravitch, historian of education, asserts that the struggle "to decide what children in school should learn and how they should be taught" began at the very inception of public education and continues today (15). Early efforts at public education consistently excluded women, the poor, immigrants, and people of color. Many marginalized communities have continuously fought for access *into and within* these institutions and have built their own when necessary.

The vision for public schooling has never been clear. Noah Webster saw great possibility in being able to instill in students a common vision of the country. Later, John Dewey, like Thomas Jefferson, saw education as a means to create an informed public, thereby preventing tyranny. The idea that public education would help students develop as citizens and normalize a particular set of behaviors conducive to a democracy connects these disparate understandings. Schools have been recognized as much for their ability to educate as they are known for their ability to control. As Louis Althusser has argued, schools can function as institutions that reproduce power structures (50–51). Schools name, present, and promote particular behaviors and epistemologies among students, teachers, and communities. The inherent power and peril in public schooling lies in its promises for educating and preparing citizens.

The experiences of the Black community with regard to citizenship and education often differ from the experience of the majority. Since the arrival of slaves in the Americas, access to literacy and language has represented power.[1] However, acquisition of literacy has not remedied all problems of injustice. Beyond struggle and oppression, both Black adults and children have worked valiantly to provide our communities with access to educational opportunities when all else seemed to fail. A look at recovery work in rhetoric and composition and literacy studies since the late 1990s (Enoch, *Refiguring*; Prendergast, *Literacy*; Gold, *Rhetoric*; Logan, *Liberating*; Moss, *Community Text*; Schneider, *You Can't*; Wan, *Producing*) demonstrates the interdisciplinary effort to understand histories of rhetoric and literacy for groups that were long ignored by mainstream scholarship. This scholarship has helped us to interrogate master narratives about literacy, race, and citizenship.

The belief that access to literacy can offer an opportunity for full participation in a democracy presents a history of struggles, as access is often met with legally sanctioned opposition and empty promises. As Harvey J. Graff has advanced through theories about the *literacy myth*, literacy has long been associated with benefiting both individuals and nations, as it contributes to developing knowledge, order, and democratic participation. However, who benefits is not always clear. Graff's discussion on the history of literacy demonstrates the kind of moral progress that is often promoted about what literacy can do for a society. Graff writes, "The power of the literacy myth lies in the first place in its resiliency, durability, and persistence. It serves to organize, simultaneously focus but obscure, and offer an explanation for an impressive array of social, economic, and political assumptions, expectations, observations, and theories on the one hand, and institutions, policies, and their workings, on the other hand" ("Literacy Myth" 643). The narrative most Americans are presented with depicts literacy as holding out the promise of progress. Graff complicates this narrative, offering a darker reading of literacy and its possibilities for damaging effects: "Perhaps the literacy myth expresses a hope that literacy alone is enough to end poverty, elevate human dignity, and promote a just and democratic world" (644). The problem becomes that, by attributing social and economic inequality to literacy, Western society obscures the real causes of poverty and oppression.

Graff's critical reading does not mean to suggest that literacy is unequivocally useless for preparation of an engaged citizenry, nor do I. We cannot discredit the desire found in marginalized communities to obtain access and training in reading, writing, and speaking for advancement, but we do need to understand how this desire is met or is not. For the Black community, literacy has traditionally represented power. As Stephen Schneider has illustrated, literacy education "would prove to be an agency for community organization and rhetorical education in its own right" (10). This certainly would hold true for the Free School. Elaine Richardson's detailed and thorough entry on African American literacies in the *Encyclopedia of Language and Education* describes literacy practices that come from within the community and delineates the primary goals of literacy for the Black community. Richardson writes, "Literacy for people of African descent is the ability to accurately read their experiences of being in the world with others and to act on this knowledge in a manner beneficial for self-preservation, economic, spiritual, and cultural uplift" (340). A look at scholarship in literacy and writing studies reflects what Richardson describes. From the Sea Island Citizenship Schools to the Black Panther Party's educational platform, literacy has not made white supremacy disappear, but it has certainly challenged its power. Literacy then means much more than learning to write one's name or read a job advertisement; literacy is a means of survival, growth, and countering injustices. Free School administrators and teachers were invested in literacy as being an opportunity to provide skills for these students and a way to counter the ideologies and arguments that dominated their communities.

Considerable scholarship in our field has recovered histories of rhetoric and literacy instruction designed for marginalized communities. Jacqueline Jones Royster's foreword to Elaine B. Richardson and Ronald L. Jackson's 2004 *African American Rhetoric(s): Interdisciplinary Perspectives* called for "a recovery of achievements and legacies," as well as research that would "address directly and specifically complex pedagogical problems" (x). This project seeks to answer the call to explore the range of rhetorical and literacy practices the Black community has employed to resist oppression. Many of the recovered histories in rhetoric and literacy studies illuminate the complicated alliance between literacy and citizenship for groups that have been systematically marginalized from democratic participation. Susan Kates has recounted how responsive curricula and pedagogies have helped marginalized groups confront sexism, racism, and classism. Jessica Enoch's work examining the rhetorical education women teachers employed for Black, Native American, and Chicano/a students in the late nineteenth and early twentieth century helped us to see how these curricula supported students' civic participation in the public sphere. David Gold's recovery of literacy practices and rhetorical educations has challenged our understanding of the relationship between conservative practices and ideologies, arguing that current traditional practices of teaching reading, writing, and speaking do not always oppress students. Jacqueline Jones Royster's pathbreaking examination of nineteenth-century African American women's literacy practices sheds light on a group often erroneously assumed to have had limited literacy. Further, Shirley Wilson Logan has pointed to the importance of understanding sites outside of the traditional—literary societies, Black newspapers, places of worship, and military camps—to demonstrate the multifarious ways in which the Black community has acquired and used language. Carmen Kynard's formative investigation of Black freedom movements in relation to literacy further expands our understanding of literacy in the Black community.

Such rich accounts have allowed us to realize that literacy is more than a set of skills given (or denied) to individuals; literacy also includes practices that represent powerful ideologies that are often connected to citizenship. Scholars such as Amy Wan have now called us to interrogate the history of citizenship and literacy instruction. In *Producing Good Citizens: Literacy Training in Anxious Times*, she argues that scholars in rhetoric and composition have not fully defined or theorized literacy's connection to citizenship and that citizenship "serves as shorthand for a variety of objectives in the writing classroom" (30). Wan's historical analysis recognizes the ways that literacy has been marked as not only a necessary pathway to citizenship but also a restriction. While we have a more robust understanding of how literacy practices have been developed, taught, and employed across communities that have faced systemic oppression, our job now, as Wan suggests, is to continue to interrogate literacy's coupling with citizenship as we work toward the development of curricula and pedagogies that are beneficial for citizens of the twenty-first century. In other words, we must continue to grapple with the question Bradford Stull raised in *Amid the Fall, Dreaming of Eden: Du Bois, King, Malcolm X, and Emancipatory Composition*: "Can composition (literacy) serve the creation of a just society?" (5). I believe the Free School provides us with a historical response that has contemporary implications for answering this question.

This book continues the work of scholarship in rhetoric and composition and literacy studies that has presented us with windows into the complicated relationship between literacy, citizenship, and the Black community. In this, my work responds to calls for more nuanced histories of literacy that unpack the hope, possibilities, and difficulties in responding to systemic racism through literacy. The Free School is a site where important rhetorical work took place. Its mission statements, philosophies, and curricular guides served not only as documents that guided outcomes and policy but also as arguments against racialized constructions of citizenship in Prince Edward County. Two key questions guided this project in responding to these calls: How was citizenship constructed and contested rhetorically? How did teachers from the Free School teach and encourage marginalized students to become citizens?

Chapter 1 frames the 1959–64 school closures by presenting background on Prince Edward County's earliest struggles with race and the Black community's access to education. I introduce the key theoretical concepts this project investigates: rhetoric, citizenship, and literacy. These terms are pivotal to understanding how the Free School functioned as a response to Virginia's discourse of Massive Resistance and to comprehending the role of the Free School's institutional rhetoric and praxis against systemic racism.

To understand the Free School as an institutional response, one must first understand the arguments and actions to which it responded. In chapter 2 I utilize archival sources to present and analyze the white communities' varying levels of resistance to the *Brown* ruling and the Black response to this resistance on both the national and local levels. By the early 1960s, the Massive Resistance effort had subsided in most parts of the South, but Virginia's social and political leadership continued to uphold laws and a climate of resistance. The closing of Prince Edward's schools depended on this continued effort. Chapter 2 presents an analysis of the key rhetorical tactics used by leading segregationists throughout Virginia.

Segregationist arguments and the school closures did not meet silence or passive acceptance on the part of the Black community. The second half of chapter 2 presents an analysis of the grassroots efforts of the Black church, community organizers, and allies. In particular, the partnership between the Black community and the American Friends Service Committee (AFSC), part of the Quaker religious organization, would eventually lead to President Kennedy's awareness of the plight of Prince Edward's children. I will argue that the Free School's response had much in common with the protest movements of the civil rights era that centered on respectability and access.

Chapter 3 presents the Free School's curricular goals for literacy and pedagogical practices as responses to the segregationists' rhetoric of resistance. This chapter focuses on documents present in the Free School archive. Through the analysis of central documents (handbooks, statement of philosophy, accreditation materials, and curricular guides) I demonstrate how Free School teachers and administrators designed programs to support reading, writing, and speaking that were reflections of their desire to speak back to the institutional structures and powers that kept schools closed. In my review of archival materials, three themes emerged that speak to how teachers and administrators attempted to make this possible. These include: demonstrating respect for students, instruction in Standard English that welcomed students' individual expressions of language and identity, and pedagogical practices that supported and encouraged a variety of ways for students to practice civic participation. These curricular goals and aims were quite similar to those found in segregated Black schools, where teachers believed it their duty to create school systems and opportunities that emphasized the importance of teacher/student relationships and affirmed the students' ability to learn despite the arguments white educators often made about Black children (Walker 200).

The Free School had a vision to teach students "to think and observe carefully" and "formulate answers that are important to our civilization" (Sullivan, "Prince Edward County Free School Association" [Handbook]). To realize this vision, teachers and administrators had to continually negotiate how to meet these goals inside the school, realizing that the school itself was part of a larger community in Prince Edward. There was general support among Free School faculty for the founding mission to create thoughtful, active citizens, but administrators and teachers did not always agree on the praxis necessary to sustain this commitment. Both groups struggled to define and practice a literacy curriculum with culturally relevant pedagogy that could respond to the argument that public civility in southern communities depended on segregation. Conversations reflected in various archival materials reveal both the tensions and challenges involved in establishing curricula and engaging pedagogies that were responsive to the needs of students and mindful of the power white supremacist ideologies held in this community.

While archival documents represent an abundance of formal institutional guidance, and reports teachers completed twice each term describe their experiences in the classroom, the voices of students are thin. Chapter 4 presents student responses that appear through teachers' reflections and contemporary interviews with students who attended the Free School. I work to present a more holistic sense of what the experience was like for some students, as understanding the students' experiences through the information teachers recorded can be problematic. In this chapter I note themes that surface across both the archive and interviews. First, students recognized the school as a response to Massive Resistance. Second, teachers and administrators at the Free School had to work hard to earn the trust of students.

I conclude with reflections on the contemporary implications of this history and analysis. The Free School offers an example of both curricular and pedagogical responses to political powers and systemic oppression. The unfortunate situation parents and youth in Prince Edward faced is unlikely to occur in the United States again, but the Free School's response does have significance for those committed to antiracist pedagogies, literacy instruction as preparation for citizenship, and programmatic design that responds to institutional racism. The Free School's story reaffirms the inherent power and hope that literacy has held for many marginalized communities; however, it also demonstrates the harsh reality that literacy alone does not solve the problem of inequality and systemic racism. The idea of literacy as a magic remedy, which contemporary scholars and communities have dismissed has waned. We are now challenged to see how the literacy myth perpetuates ideologies and systems that further secure literacy as a gatekeeping function. The hopefulness of communities that turned to literacy as a response to or action against oppression supports a fuller understanding of the limitations and possibilities of literacy instruction as part of the remedy for systemic oppressions.

1

Rhetoric, Race, and Citizenship in the Heart of Virginia

Can the study of composition (literacy) serve the creation of a just commonwealth? If it can, how can it? What might emancipatory composition, a composition meant to set free the captives and give sight to the blind, be?

BRADFORD STULL, *AMID THE FALL, DREAMING OF EDEN*

[I]f we are to understand the nature of citizenship since 1957, and its requirements, we need to analyze the moment of desegregation, when the polity was coming unstitched and rewoven.

DANIELLE S. ALLEN, *TALKING TO STRANGERS*

On the evening of Sunday, September 15, 1963, many Black parents in Prince Edward County were preparing to send their children to school for the first time in four years. That same day, the Sixteenth Street Baptist Church bombing in Birmingham, Alabama, killed four young girls and injured many more. The news of the deaths from the fifteen sticks of dynamite Ku Klux Klan members had set in a place of worship shook the nation. Like the summer that preceded this horrific event, it marked a turning point in the civil rights movement. White supremacist violence at this level had not reached Prince Edward County and never did, but parents whose children would attend the opening day of the Free School on September 16 had no way of knowing that it would not. After four years with no public education, no one knew what to expect.

The September 16, 1963, issue of the *Richmond Afro-American* covered the story of the school's opening alongside a column on the bombing. The civil rights movement often generated emotional highs and lows in short periods of time. This juxtaposition is highlighted by the newspaper's stories on the devastation and deaths in Birmingham, with one article calling that city a "hell hole" and, beside it, another describing the "happiness and excitement" of the Black community for the Free School's opening day ("Opening Day Ceremonies"). This first day of school was possible because of a culmination of struggle, persuasion, and steadfast belief that it was possible to restore educational opportunities to Prince Edward's Black citizens.

Few court cases involving public education have garnered the attention and recognition of the *Brown v. Board of Education* rulings (1954, 1955). *Brown* ended separate but equal schooling on paper, ruling it unconstitutional. The doctrine of separate but equal had permitted state-sponsored segregation in public schools since the 1896 *Plessy v. Ferguson* ruling, but the act of separation based on color was well established by both law and custom. Segregation had been the order of the day since slavery was instituted, as a means to uphold and protect the interests of plantation owners, and this lawful separation continued through numerous laws enacted after emancipation. *Plessy v. Ferguson* bolstered Jim Crow and Black codes by upholding state-sanctioned segregation based on race.

Prior to *Brown*, the National Association for the Advancement of Colored People (NAACP) used the separate but equal doctrine to realize a number of legal victories that resulted in equal resource allocation to segregated schools in particular localities, but town-by-town legal battles quickly drained resources. Further, segregated schools had never been equal. NAACP executive secretary Lester Banks announced the need to press for integration as the only way for the Black community to "achieve their full dignity as citizens," and as early as 1935 NAACP lawyers were building a legal strategy to support this effort (Kluger 477).[1] As the United States sought to cultivate a reputation for supporting democracy around the world through its involvement in World Wars I and II, deeming this impression a critical weapon in the Cold War, the Black community demanded an end to the second-class status the separate but equal doctrine forced upon them.

The Supreme Court acknowledged through the *Brown* decision that segregation caused Black children to be deprived: "Segregation of white and colored children in public schools has a detrimental effect upon the colored children. . . . A sense of inferiority affects the motivation of a child to learn" (Brown v. Board I 494). The ruling recognized the connection between public schooling and citizenship preparation: "Today, education is perhaps the most important function of state and local governments. . . . It is required in the performance of our most basic public responsibilities, even service in the armed forces. It is the very foundation of good citizenship" (493). Citizenship, in this instance, was described as a role that could be attained through skill sets that could be offered in public schooling. While citizenship has myriad definitions, for the purposes of this book I am interested in the skills or traits that schools have historically offered students in a quest to groom young people for democratic life. Wan writes that "educative spaces have always been positioned as crucial elements of citizenship production," but these spaces do not always thoroughly define what is meant by citizenship and how literacy helps one to achieve this status (17). Calling out the "ambient nature of the term 'citizenship,'" Wan builds on Graff's work as she reminds us that without careful examination of what *kind* of citizenship is being sought after, or achieved, or what kind of literacy skills are believed to get one to that role, we fall short of unpacking "the implicit understanding that equality and social mobility are synonymous with and can be achieved through citizenship" (18). Part of understanding the ways in which literacy has been yoked to preparation necessary for citizenship comes from examining moments when education has been believed to be a way to "alleviate anxieties" during economic, social, or national moments of anxiety (Wan 16). As *Brown* sought to address the issue of segregation and inequality, it also expressed a reminder that public education was necessary for citizenship.

Prince Edward County's board of supervisors responded to *Brown* through what they believed to be an expression of citizenship. Their statement, published in the county's newspaper, expressed a desire to meet the needs of *all* the county's citizens: "It is with the most profound regret that we have been compelled to take this action. . . . [I]t is the fervent hope of this board that . . . we may in due time be able to resume the operation of public schools in this county upon a basis acceptable to all the people of the county" (qtd. in Smith 151). This response reveals their fear of the impact *Brown* could have on those invested in maintaining control over the Black community.

Brown, at its core, was about securing through integration the same educational resources and opportunities for Black students that whites already enjoyed; however, the ruling did not supply a framework for the unraveling of segregation. Thurgood Marshall, head NAACP lawyer for the *Brown* case, told news outlets that he was "cautiously optimistic" about the ruling; he said that if white people tried to defy the high court "in the morning, we'll have them in court the next morning—or possibly that same afternoon" (qtd. in Pratt 3). The second *Brown* ruling, delivered in May 1955, attempted to provide guidance for implementation, calling for an end to segregation with "all deliberate speed" (Brown v. Board II 301), but this proclamation was vague with regard to procedure and process, and white resistance became palpable both in the streets and in the state legislatures. As I recount here, in Prince Edward County the resistance had been brewing for quite some time.

Danielle Allen contends that *Brown* triggered "anxieties of citizenship," and in the years following the *Brown* ruling US society had to consider what citizenship meant when one group was no longer systematically and legally excluded from participating with the majority (4). As the epigraph to this chapter suggests, *Brown* redefined both public education and citizenship. The *Brown* ruling, its precipitating events, and responses to it reveal the full spectrum of discourse on constructions of American citizenship.

Catherine Prendergast argues that the post-*Brown* era did not live up to its expectations, and she asserts that the high court's decision reflects thinking "on a grand scale that the rationale in *Brown* for ending legalized segregation rested on defining public education as the precursor to good citizenship" (17). She acknowledges the connection the ruling made between citizenship and education; however, Prendergast challenges the ways in which *Brown* reified literacy as a "white property," thus continuing to damage the prospect of racial justice and social reform. Her argument holds that an understanding of literacy as a set of transferable skills, which can be granted to or shared with marginalized communities by those in power, does little to advance social justice. Prendergast demonstrates that "throughout American history, literacy has been managed and controlled in a variety of ways to rationalize and ensure white domination" (2). Whether this happened through laws forbidding slaves to learn to read and write or through the unequal allocation of funding for segregated schools, literacy has been a means by which whites can exert control over Black communities. Post-*Brown* Prince Edward County exemplified this stance, as white community leaders continued to take it upon themselves to control access to education and to prescribe what citizenship could and could not look like for Black people. The Free School's restoration of free public education to the community was another endeavor to challenge these ideologies.[2]

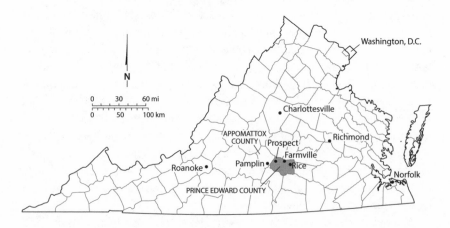

Figure 1. Map of Prince Edward County and surrounding areas. Map by William Nelson, Cartographer

A History of Prince Edward County's Battle for Equal Education

Prince Edward County sits sixty miles southwest of Richmond, the capital of Virginia, in the center of the state. This rural, central Virginia county was formed in 1754. Much of the county's prosperity in its first century came from the rich cash crop of tobacco, but plantations also produced wheat, corn, dairy products, and livestock (Adams and Rainey 47). Early relationships between Blacks and whites as slaves and masters varied across the region. While slavery was assuredly the norm of the day, historians have discovered that there were some anomalies. The owner of Bizarre plantation near Farmville, Richard Randolph released the slaves he had been given by his father. Randolph's will declared the evils of slavery, "expressing . . . abhorrence of the theory, as well as [the] infamous practice, of usurping the rights of our fellow creatures, equally entitled with ourselves to the enjoyment of liberty and happiness" (qtd. in Adams and Rainey 49). Randolph's slaves, freed in 1796, would settle on a parcel of land at Bizarre known as Israel Hill, making "the Farmville community unique among antebellum southern towns" because of its large number of free Blacks before emancipation (Adams and Rainey 50).[3] Before the Civil War the 1860 census reported that 44 percent of the population was made up of whites, 16 percent free Blacks, and slaves made up the remaining 40 percent (Adams and Rainey 51). The population demographics would remain relatively consistent throughout the middle of the twentieth century, with whites finding themselves in the minority. According to data collected by the US Census Bureau in 1950, the population of Prince Edward County was 15,398, with 55 percent (8,538) listed as white and 45 percent (6,860) as nonwhite. In 1960, the Census Bureau indicated that population of Prince Edward had decreased to 14,121. However, the percentage of the population listed as white increased to 60 percent (8,488), and the nonwhite population decreased to 40 percent (5,633). Of the nonwhite population, all but two individuals were listed as Black (US Census 1950 46–86; US Census 1960 48–65).

While freedom on paper would come for the Black community with the Emancipation Proclamation in 1863, the Reconstruction and post-Reconstruction eras found many free Blacks facing the challenge of navigating their newfound freedom in the face of continued social stratification across the South, and Prince Edward was no different. In part, the Civil Rights Act of 1866 and the Fourteenth and Fifteenth Amendments, respectively, were rendered useless with *Plessy v. Ferguson*'s affirmation of Jim Crow laws that maintained white control through segregation.

A visit to Farmville by W. E. B. Du Bois in July 1897 led to a report titled "The Negroes of Farmville, Virginia: A Social Study." Du Bois detailed the community's attempts to be self-sustaining and independent in the face of segregation.

He reported that there were no Black schools in Farmville. Instead, there was a district school operating in the county. The school, with one male principal and four assistants, was considered unsuccessful because of its lack of resources and teachers. There were few work opportunities in Farmville, with many in the county working the land to feed their families. In spite of these conditions, Du Bois noted, there was an "adjusted interdependence" between Blacks and whites (23). In part, this adjusted interdependence represented the types of relationships between Blacks and whites in many rural localities where agricultural work often required joint effort, no matter the color of one's skin. Prince Edward was no different, with farming neighbors often helping one another at harvest time, no matter their skin color (Berryman).

Nonetheless, Jim Crow kept public spaces separated. As in most communities, while separate schools in Prince Edward meant inferior conditions for Black students, that did not always mean teachers who were not dedicated and motivated enough to have their pupils learn or parents who did not rally to support the education of their children. Vanessa Siddle Walker's careful analysis of segregated Black schools has demonstrated that "history most often focuses on the inferior education that African American children received" (1). Rather, "historical recollections that recall descriptions of differences in facilities and resources of white and Black schools without also providing descriptions of the Black schools' and communities dogged determination to educate African American children have failed to tell the complete story of segregated schools and the parental and community support African American children did have" (4–5). Kara Miles Turner's work does just that for Prince Edward. In "'Getting It Straight': Southern Black School Patrons and the Struggle for Equal Education in the Pre-and Post-Civil Rights Eras," she details the numerous instances in which Black parents in Prince Edward sought improvements in their children's schools, including repairing buildings, longer school terms, and transportation. Early county records, predating Du Bois's visit, show that Blacks steadily petitioned the school board for better teachers and resources for their schools. In 1882, a county school board report described six Black citizens of the county who had petitioned the school board in Farmville for colored teachers who were as competent as those in the white schools. The school board denied this request. Prior to the late 1930s, the county required Black parents to subsidize teachers' salaries to keep their schools open as many days as white schools stayed open with full state funding (Turner, "'Getting'" 221). Parents contributed out of pocket the funds for books and building maintenance while also footing the bill for white students through their county taxes. These inequalities continued well into the middle of the twentieth century before the Black community reached its tipping point.

On April 23, 1951, students at Robert Russa Moton High School, the county's only Black high school, planned and executed a walkout under the leadership of sixteen-year-old Barbara Rose Johns.[4] Protesting the poor conditions of the schools, the students would meet with the superintendent and county school board to voice their frustrations. Oliver Hill and Spottswood Robinson, lawyers from Richmond's NAACP, came to Farmville to investigate, and the NAACP filed suit. In the filing for *Davis v. County School Board of Prince Edward County* the plaintiffs demanded school desegregation, calling "separate but equal" a sham. The NAACP combined the case with four others: *Briggs v. Elliott* (South Carolina), *Gebhart v. Belton* (Delaware), *Bolling v. Sharpe* (Washington, DC), and *Brown v. Board of Education* (Kansas); combined, they would come to be known as *Brown*. The Prince Edward Black community's involvement in the quest for equitable education was present from the beginning of the civil rights era, as was resistance from the white community.

The county's journey toward negating the *Brown* ruling began in April 1955. Members of the Defenders of State Sovereignty and Individual Liberties, a group formed to protect segregation, visited the Prince Edward County Board of Supervisors to voice their opposition to integrated schools. The Defenders were spread across Virginia but had an especially large membership in Prince Edward because the group's president, Robert Crawford, was a local business owner. Defenders also sat on the county's board of supervisors. In *Brown's Battleground: Students, Segregationists, and the Struggle for Justice in Prince Edward County, Virginia*, the historian Jill Ogline Titus describes as "pillars of the community" these men who told the board that they would not support taxes that contributed to integrated schools. They were able to sway the board to postpone a decision on the budget. The following month, on May 31, 1955, when *Brown* II was released and "all deliberate speed" became the threat to segregation, concerned white citizens once more approached the board to ask them to halt any appropriation of funding for schools. Board members acquiesced and passed only a small operating budget—enough to cover building upkeep but not enough to operate a school system (Titus 27).

Meanwhile, in June 1955 the Prince Edward Educational Corporation was established. This corporation's goal was to ensure private, segregated education for white children in the event of forced integration and school closures. Within the summer the corporation raised $180,000 in pledges, surpassing the monthly budget being allotted for the entire Prince Edward County public school system. Public schools would reopen for the 1955–56 school year, but the corporation kept its pledges, just in case alternative schooling was necessary (Titus 30).

At the close of the 1956 school year, white residents would once more voice their support for limiting the budget of the public school system as a precautionary measure against the threat of integration. The May 3, 1956, public hearing on the county's budget for the 1956–57 school year was met with support when board members voted to continue passing a heretofore policy, which meant that it passed a budget for only thirty days at a time (Titus 30). That same evening, the county's board of supervisors received a "Declaration of Convictions" signed by more than four thousand white citizens of Prince Edward. The manifesto acknowledged their support for the abandonment of public schools should integration become mandatory, citing their preference to "abandon public schools and educate our children in some other way if that is necessary to preserve segregation of the races in the schools of the county" (qtd. in Titus 31). Segregated schools would continue to operate for the 1956–57 and 1957–58 school years.

Prince Edward's proponents for segregation felt some level of reprieve when a district court judge, Sterling Hutcheson, ruled that Prince Edward would have until September 1965 to comply with the desegregation order. Judge Hutcheson, from the Fourth District Court, referenced his knowledge of the area and culture, rather than legal precedent, in what was clearly a departure from *Brown* II. When the state's Court of Appeals reversed his opinion in 1958, Hutcheson ruled that Prince Edward could have until 1965 to integrate. The Fourth Circuit Court of Appeals reversed the ruling once more in 1959, ordering Prince Edward to desegregate its schools immediately. That move triggered the backup plan that many of Prince Edward's white citizens had for years been conspiring to develop. It was at this point when Prince Edward County's board of supervisors refused to allocate funds for public schools for any child. On June 2, 1959, Prince Edward County's school board announced the closure of all public schools. They reasoned that "[t]he action taken today has been determined upon only after the most careful and deliberate study over the long period of years since the schools in this county were first brought under the force of federal court decree. It is with the most profound regret that we have been compelled to take this action. It is the fervent hope of this board that we may in due time be able to resume the operation of public schools in this county upon a basis acceptable to all the people of the county" (qtd. in Smith 151).

For the white community, the cessation of public schooling caused little disruption to most students' day-to-day activities. The private segregated Prince Edward Academy established by the corporation would fulfill the needs of most white students. For those who were unable to afford the tuition, the state's tuition grants and local scholarship funding helped to cover the cost. The Black community pulled together resources as quickly as possible to mitigate the effects of the school closure on their students.

As will be shown in the next chapter, the Black community took a number of steps to help ensure that the education of Black children would continue, but the Free School represented the first effort by the federal government to reintroduce free public schooling for both Black and white children. The Free School Association would be different from the freedom schools that developed during the civil rights movement because of its affiliation with the federal government and the context in which it was founded; however, both alternative school systems shared similar pedagogical strategies. Freedom schools, developed in part by Charles Cobb and the Student Nonviolent Coordinating Committee (SNCC) to meet their political and educational objectives, served Black children. With a focus on leadership skills, Black history, and activism, the schools' ultimate aim was to provide youth an opportunity to develop as citizens who could effect change through the civil rights movement and who could contribute to the challenging constructions of race. The Free School's administrators sought to avoid making overt statements about race or their connection to the civil rights movement, although I will argue that their very existence was in fact a statement about race and was part of the legacy of the civil rights movement and its education goals.

I argue for the Free School to be seen as a response to the rhetorical context in which Massive Resistance emerged in Virginia. Histories of institutional rhetoric matter to rhetoric, composition, and literacy studies because of how they expand our understanding of programmatic design and response. I aim to extend these conversations by looking not only at the literacy curriculum and pedagogical practices of the school (specifically, the literacy program) but at the school itself as a rhetorical response to the rhetorics of Massive Resistance.

Methods and Methodology

To answer these questions, I have used historical, archival, rhetorical listening and analysis, and structured interview methods. This project incorporates primary sources from three archives. The Free School Association archive is housed at Virginia State University (formerly Virginia State College) in Ettrick, Virginia. All of the papers from the Free School were donated to this university's Johnston Memorial Library archive after the summer of 1964. Dr. Robert P. Daniel, president of Virginia State College and a trustee of the Free School, helped to orchestrate the acquisition of the artifacts after the Free School year ended.[5] The archives accessed for materials relating to Sen. Harry F. Byrd Sr. are housed at the University of Virginia's Albert and Shirley Small Special Collections Library. From this archive I obtained Byrd's speeches, public statements, press releases, and correspondence relating to Massive Resistance. Primary source materials on the Defenders of State Sovereignty and Individual Liberties, the grassroots political organization in Virginia that supported the Massive Resistance movement, came from the Library of Virginia. The Library of Virginia also served as the primary repository for articles from the *Richmond Times-Dispatch* (the morning newspaper), *Richmond News Leader* (the afternoon newspaper), and the *Farm-*

ville Herald. These sources were critical for providing news and editorials from this time period. As is the case for most who do historical work, my project was directly shaped by the holdings of these archives.

The historical methods employed were directed by a desire to understand the ways in which teachers and administrators were responding to the needs of the Black community through educational resources. In this, I follow Robert Connors's practice of using contemporary events to ask questions about the past: "What has been done in the past [for similar circumstances]? How did things come to be this way?" (17). Moving from general questions such as the ones Connors suggests, I constructed questions generated from the documents I read during my first archive visit as well as from the knowledge I received through family stories: What did a literacy program look like in the Free School? How did the federal government's involvement affect the curriculum and the way the school was received within both the Black and white communities? How would a community that had been without public education respond to this school and its mission? What did education look like in a space where students were being legally denied the right to attend school? How was the curriculum designed, enacted, and received? What effect did the curriculum have on both teachers and students? How were the teachers (who came from around the country and had a wide range of backgrounds) trained to provide this type of education through professional development opportunities? While I had a host of questions, I also understood that archives do not always provide us with all of the answers. Understanding then that we must often build history from what Jan Swearingen called "shards" is important for those writing histories (Murphy et al. 23). Despite the inherent difficulty of working with shards, if we are to expand our histories of rhetoric we must work patiently with what we are able to find. In this project, I did so by combining methods: archival materials, historiography, and interviews. In the section that follows, I describe each of the methods separately, for purposes of clarity. There was certainly overlap and connectivity between how I worked through each, especially with regard to how the interviews influenced my understanding of what was found in the archive, which I explain at the end.

The Free School holdings consist of fifty thousand items and contain everything from bus schedules, handbooks, textbook orders, teacher applications, textbook order forms, curricula guides, varsity jackets, personnel files, and faculty handbooks to lunch menus. The documents and materials were categorized by type (memos, teaching handbooks, receipts, etc.) and further organized in chronological order. I utilized the University of Virginia's Special Collections archives to access Senator Byrd's papers. To examine his arguments, I read a host of speeches, notes, and letters written from 1954 to 1964 and selected the most representative of the arguments he made during the Massive Resistance era. The

Defenders archive was the smallest of the three and consisted of several pamphlets and some recruitment materials, all produced in the same ten-year period.

My work within each of the archives began with rhetorical listening. This listening is influenced by the theories Krista Ratcliffe advances in *Rhetorical Listening: Identification, Gender, and Whiteness*. Ratcliffe maintains that rhetorical listening "signifies a stance of openness that a person may choose to assume in relation to any person, text, or culture" (1). While Ratcliffe's primary focus is rhetorical listening to aid cross-cultural understanding, in particular with regard to conversations about race and gender, this type of listening, as the definition implies, can be used with any text or person to open the door for understanding (17).

Ratcliffe describes four moves as being part of successfully enacting the pragmatic elements of rhetorical listening. Of these four, I found one to be most fitting for my work in the archives. In the first move she differentiates between the actions of listening and understanding as we commonly understand them: "*understanding* means listening to discourses not *for* intent but *with* intent—with the intent to understand not just the claims but the rhetorical negotiations of understanding as well" (28). For Ratcliffe this type of understanding means that one "stands under" discourses to see how they affect ourselves and others (29). With regard to my own work, this practice has meant that as I read documents from decades ago, I acknowledge that they existed within their own time and rhetorical context. To try to avoid placing my own paradigms upon them, I worked to listen to the items on their own terms.

Lynée Lewis Gaillet describes a similar process of listening to archival material and understanding the importance of context as a series of tasks and questions related to evaluating materials (33). Of the tasks she lists, what I found most essential for my own process of listening and understanding context was framing materials "within political, social, economic, educational, religious, or institutional histories of the time" (35). This process meant careful cross-referencing and consulting multiple secondary sources to learn more about Prince Edward County's involvement in the civil rights movement, literacy education during the middle of the twentieth century, educational histories, and politics surrounding resistance to *Brown*. To be able to analyze the documents in the archives, I needed to understand the cultural moment in which the audience was receiving these messages. While my primary method for gaining understanding of the conversations and themes that emerged across the archives involved consulting secondary sources on Black and white experiences after *Brown*, I also placed the materials in conversation with the stories and experiences gathered from the interviews I conducted. Ratcliffe's fourth move in the process of rhetorical listening, the process of examining claims within their own cultural logic, is quite similar to the type of cross-referencing and locating that Gaillet describes.

Ratcliffe writes, "[I]f a claim is an assertion of a person's thinking, then a cultural logic is a belief system or shared way of reasoning within which a claim may function" (33). Adopting this stance as a guide was especially important for me while I listened and traced conversations in the archives, because it reminded me to historicize and contextualize the conversations and themes I found. Historicizing and contextualizing meant not only trying to frame the pieces within a particular time period but also understanding their rhetorical situation. Working to understand the cultural logics that surrounded the artifacts was integral to understanding both the claims presented and their connections to larger arguments about rhetoric, race, citizenship, and literacy. As we work to both represent and analyze historical moments, we must also be aware that this too is an exercise in rhetoric.

While Ratcliffe's method is described as a possible means of establishing better cross-cultural communication, I believe that it holds useful strategies for those engaged in historical research as well. We are listening to artifacts, trying to place them in their proper historical context and rhetorical situation, but doing so requires consistent self-reflexivity on our own part. Ratcliffe notes, "By championing a responsibility logic, rhetorical listening asks us, first, to judge not simply the person's intent but the historically situated discourses that are (un) consciously swirling around and through the person and, second, to evaluate politically and ethically how these discourses function and [how] we want to act upon them" (207). Being willing to place the artifacts within their rhetorical situation and proper historical moment was integral to understanding the conversations and themes that emerged across the archive, as well as to how I was understanding them as being part of larger conversations about histories of race, literacy, citizenship, and education.

While the archives I worked in were discrete collections, their contents often spoke to one another. Katherine Tirabassi's description of cross-referencing provided four key principles for archival work, two of which were essential for how I worked across multiple boxes and folders: cross-referencing (searching across the documents for clues or clarification with regard to the rhetorical situation of a document) and closure (the understanding that there are going to be gaps in archival materials and that one must find an entrance and exit point) (171–72). Cross-referencing (pairing newspaper articles with memos, for example) enabled me to understand historical contexts and to begin to trace conversations as they arose from the materials. I was also conscious of the need to pay attention to the gaps and silences found in the archive; for example, the lack of direct student voices in the archive prompted me to include interviews in this project.

Interviews with former Free School students established a valuable pathway into the research. Their perspectives offer firsthand information on what the

Free School year was like for some. Since the Free School's archive held very little, I am careful to represent these personal accounts as individual experiences and not to advance the notion that they are representative of all who attended. To conduct these interviews, I relied on standard interview techniques. My interviews were conducted with the intention of "understand[ing] themes of the lived daily world from the subjects' own perspectives" (Kvale and Brinkmann 24). In total, I interviewed seven former students with five being able to recollect time and experiences at the Free School. All but one are still residents of Prince Edward County or the surrounding area, and all are active in their community in a variety of roles. Three responded to an advertisement I placed in a local community newsletter and two responded through familial connections. On average, each interview lasted between thirty and forty minutes. Most interviews began with me sharing both my familial and academic genealogies. I used a set of pre-established questions for each session. Participants recalled their experiences both before the schools closed and during their Free School year. As I will show in chapter 4, listening to the histories and experiences of these participants enriched the themes that surfaced in the archive.

To understand the rhetorics employed to close the schools and establish the Free School year, I adopted, in addition to the type of listening theorized by Ratcliffe, an analytical framework that helps to uncover how arguments were constructed to promote such actions. To analyze the arguments made by segregationists in the white community, I rely on theories from whiteness studies and historians of southern identity that seek to explicate how the white community benefits from constructs of race that have historically placed them in dominant positions over the Black community, as well as rhetorical theories that seek to explain how groups create and maintain group identities in social movements (Lipsitz, *Possessive*; Cobb, *Away*; Brundage, *These Memories*; Woodward, *Burden*). To explore the Black community's response, I utilize the work of scholars in African American rhetoric who demonstrate how the position of the Black community has led to language practices developed out of a need for resistance and survival (Pough, *Check It*; Gilyard, "Introduction"; Richardson and Jackson, *Understanding*; Richardson and Jackson, *Rhetoric(s)*; Royster, *Traces*; Logan, *Liberating*). These analytical frameworks will be expounded upon in chapters 2 and 3, respectively.

Reflecting on Personal and Academic Connections in Research

From the beginning, I knew that my relationship with the geographic area would provide me with access and knowledge that other researchers might not be privy to, but my relationship was also something that I would need to consistently reflect upon. I have made it a practice to be clear about my relationship to this project on both the personal and academic levels at every step in this project.

This transparency is a means by which I am able to critically question and remain aware of the commitments I maintain to two different communities.

I am not only a collector of stories, histories, and materials for this project but a granddaughter, great-niece, daughter, and cousin. Jacqueline Jones Royster's work in *Traces of a Stream* provides both a model and a reassurance. My connection to Prince Edward binds, drives, and complicates this work. I remain aware of not only the importance of this research, but the necessity of constantly reflecting on my connection and roles as researcher and community member. Royster acknowledges the complexities involved as she admits that she is unapologetically tied to the subjects she studies. Through her close examination of the position she occupies as both researcher of Black women and member of this community, she identifies one of her goals as an Afrafeminist researcher as the acknowledgment of responsibility to her community: "As African American women intellectuals doing this work, we are obligated, as are our counterparts within the community, to be holistic, to remember our connectedness in both places. We are free to do our own intellectual business and at the same time we are also obligated to have that work respond to sociopolitical imperatives that encumber the community itself" (275). Royster's methods speak to the importance of understanding how the position and stance of a researcher are critical both for writing and for the relationships we may have with the groups we study. Her acknowledgment and explanation of the "passionate attachment" she has to her work serve as an important reminder "that knowledge has sites and sources and that we are better informed about the nature of a given knowledge base when we take into account its sites, material contexts and points of origin" (280). The acknowledgment and understanding of how these *passionate attachments* work and what implications they hold are integral to both the construction of knowledge and what action may arise from it. My own process of self-reflexivity has meant acknowledging that I am both a member of the larger Prince Edward community because of my familial relations and a member of the academic community because of my training and work. This awareness is one step in practicing self-reflexivity. Throughout the process of researching and writing, I have worked to listen carefully at moments when I have felt less "holistic" or "connected" in the way Royster describes. In the instances when I felt myself moving closer toward one paradigm or way of understanding, or when I was feeling disconnected from a particular tradition of scholarship, I have reminded myself of the importance both communities hold with regard to my understanding and knowledge-making. Thus, the entirety of this project is meant to bring all of my relations into conversation about what it means to resist oppression through literacy and rhetorical traditions deeply rooted in a quest for liberation.[6]

In the next chapter, I describe how Virginia set precedents for opposition to *Brown* across the South and made Prince Edward a procreant site for defiance through careful legal and public argument strategies. If we are to understand how the Free School functioned as a response to Massive Resistance, this context matters. Further, I describe and analyze the ways in which the Black community responded to the resistance displayed by whites in Prince Edward. Prince Edward's Black community practiced many of the rhetorical strategies Blacks had developed during the civil rights movement to make sure their needs were met. The initial responses by Black Prince Edwardians focused on alleviating the damage closing schools had done and on finding alternative routes to literacy access, actions that would lay the groundwork for the Free School.

2

Manufacturing and Responding to White Supremacist Ideology the "Virginia Way"

As the bombing of Pearl Harbor was to the entire nation, so the *Brown* decision was to the white South.

ROBERT PRATT, *THE COLOR OF THEIR SKIN*

The history of southern identity is not a study of continuity versus change, but continuity within it.

JAMES COBB, *AWAY DOWN SOUTH*

I would sacrifice my job, money, and any property for the principles of right. I offered my life for a decadent democracy [in World War II], and I'm willing to die rather than let these children down.

REV. FRANCIS L. GRIFFIN, QUOTED IN RICHARD KLUGER, *SIMPLE JUSTICE*

In this chapter I analyze Massive Resistance as part of a continuum of rhetorical strategies aimed at maintaining white supremacy through racialized constructions of citizenship. I present the rhetorical context in which Prince Edward County's public schools closed by using the arguments made in support of legislative packages presented by segregationists like Sen. Harry F. Byrd Sr. and his supporters, such as the Defenders of State Sovereignty and Individual Liberties. The rhetoric of resistance Byrd and the Defenders employed mobilized an audience of responders through identification of commonly held beliefs and shared histories that continued to proffer segregation as a necessity. Through the invocation of historically shared cultural values and norms, such as states' rights and the protection of segregation as a tradition, Byrd and the Defenders built connections with an audience receptive to the rhetoric of Massive Resistance. For both the leaders of Massive Resistance and those sympathetic to their arguments, upholding segregation once more became synonymous with practicing good citizenship. These arguments were not specific to Virginia but are representative of discourse that circulated around the South in the effort to stop the implementation of *Brown*. They are important to histories of rhetoric and citizenship studies because we must understand the insidiousness of racism and how it operates if we are to better understand resistance efforts employed by the Black community.

Kenneth Burke's theory concerning the role of identification in persuasion and Michael McGee's theories on audience and social movements drive this analysis. For Burke, persuasion requires a speaker (or speakers) to first identify with their audience: "You persuade a man only insofar as you can talk his language by speech, gesture, tonality, order, image, attitude, idea, identifying your ways with his" (55). McGee contends that social movements create their audiences. The people "are not objectively real in the sense that they exist as a collective entity in nature"; rather, an advocate creates the "fiction" and "infuse[s it] with an artificial, rhetorical reality" through "the agreement of an audience" (240). If, as Burke suggests, people work out of divisions toward identification and unity through rhetoric, then McGee's claim that rhetors create their audiences suggests that both Byrd and the Defenders created and mobilized a new audience of responders through the identification of commonly held beliefs. Proponents of segregation invoked historically shared cultural values and norms to create an audience receptive to the rhetoric of Massive Resistance. These shared histories and terms functioned as ideographs: "an ordinary language term found in political discourse. It is a high-order abstraction representing collective commitment to a particular but equivocal and ill-defined normative goal" (McGee, "'Ideograph'" 15). Both Byrd and the Defenders established terms such as "liberty," "citizenship," and "tradition" as suggestive of the necessity of white dominance.

Additionally, I examine the small number of white voices who tried to speak against Massive Resistance. While this group of individuals lacked power to effect a turn in the trajectory of events, their attempts to speak against Massive Resistance help to provide a fuller picture of the rhetorical landscape. As I will demonstrate, speakers such as Byrd, the Defenders, and local citizens used alarmist rhetoric and references to historical precedents to organize state, local, and grassroots resistance and were quite successful in their efforts to gain control over Virginia's response to integration.

The second half of this chapter investigates the responses of Virginia's Black community, in particular Black Prince Edwardians, to Massive Resistance. While the Black response was not homogeneous, the responses of most exemplify communicative practices rooted in the Black freedom struggle, and they foreground the importance of the Black church as a site for both rhetorical education and mobilization for resistance. Opposition to the closures was expressed across public and private spaces such as the courts, churches, Black newspapers, and eventually in the streets of downtown Farmville. My analysis demonstrates that the Black community developed a multifaceted response system to confront both the arguments and the actions that had marginalized their community. In this, they refused the subordinate position whites presumed for them. This refusal would lead directly to the establishment of the Free School. The Black community has historically worked from a position that was marginalized, which forced its members to act as agents from a constrained physical and rhetorical standpoint. To survive in this position and to become activists for their cause, the Black community has both created their own and adopted rhetorical strategies used by the dominant group. As other scholars have chronicled, the use of the rhetorical strategies of the dominant group does not necessitate a replication or imitation of those in power but is rather "a reshaping and reinventing" of more radical practices (Bacon and McClish 19).

The Development of Southern Identity

Historians have long discussed the development and construction of a "southern identity." C. Vann Woodward's pathbreaking 1960 work, *The Burden of Southern History* (3rd ed., 2008), W. Fitzhugh Brundage's monograph *The Southern Past* (2005), and his edited collection *Where These Memories Grow: History, Memory, and Southern Identity* (2000), as well as James C. Cobb's *Away Down South: A History of Southern Identity*, all chronicle the way in which southern identity has been formulated and circulated. Brundage writes that "when southern identity is assumed to be interchangeable with white identity, much more than semantics are at stake. White claims to power, status and collective identity are advanced at the same time that black claims are undercut" (*Southern* 2). Historically, the southern identity has been centered on the role of white southern men. How the conflation of "southerner" with white identity evolved is directly linked to white supremacist ideology, power, and collective memory. To understand the rhetorics of Massive Resistance, one needs to have an understanding of constructs of southern identity because Massive Resistance sought to protect it at all costs.

The South's regional identity has long been defined by its sins and stereotypes. The southern historian C. Vann Woodward reflected, "To establish identity by reference to our faults was always simplest, for whatever their reservations about our virtues, our critics were never reluctant to concede us our vices and shortcomings" (5). One of the South's most recognizable vices has been its relationship with race. In Grace Elizabeth Hale's *Making Whiteness: The Culture of Segregation in the South, 1890–1940*, she traces the construction of white identity in the South and posits that its formation rests on two principles: "nowhere was this ambiguous middle, the contradictory, simultaneous need for race to be visible—blackness—and invisible—whiteness—more apparent than in the South. Southern whites constructed their racial identities on two interlocking planes: within a regional dynamic of ex-Confederates versus ex-slaves and within a national dynamic of the South, understood as white, versus the nation" (9). I want to be clear that the preoccupation with race is not only characteristic of the South. The entire nation has had a problem with race. The South has a special relationship with the issue because of slavery, and it has been marked in this way for better or worse.

Traditionally, southern discourse has described the role of good citizens and citizenship in a way that would benefit white men, protect white women, and advocate for a "necessary" control over Black communities for the interests of all. These themes can be traced as far back as the colonial era, when arguments were fashioned to suggest that the separation of Blacks and whites was necessary for the survival of both communities. Laws crafted to support slavery in the colonies and later the legal principles of the Constitution dictated access to freedom and narrowly defined who would count as a citizen. While the Fourteenth Amendment (1868) abolished slavery and the Fifteenth Amendment (1870) gave Black men the right to vote, legislation reflecting the Black codes and Jim Crow rules disenfranchised Blacks, making full citizenship impossible to practice. Proslavery rhetoric was often deeply rooted in religious, economic, science, and social arguments. In 1619, the first Africans were sold as cargo from Dutch ships, and by 1633 New England colonies were holding Africans in servitude. As the number of plantations grew throughout the Americas, African labor and African citizenship were clearly defined: "The institution of slavery was swiftly codified into the legal framework of colonial society and became integral to its economy" (Baker 13). Further, for slavery to develop as an institution, arguments for maintaining control over other humans were based on the idea that Blacks, by nature, were unable to govern themselves. The end of the eighteenth century brought new scientific rationales and "proofs" about race that suggested Africans were inferior and also provided fodder for those turning toward religious justifications for slavery.

The South was entrenched in a social and legal system that maintained order and profit through the institution of slavery. However, race was at once visible and invisible. Race became an unacknowledged spoke in the wheel of white control. Arguments made by the South's most prominent voices further testified to the region's wholesale investment in these citizenship roles. Jefferson Davis, who would become president of the Confederacy, articulated in an 1858 speech to the

Mississippi legislature his view that slave labor was necessary both for capital and for the very equality of white men. In this speech, he advocated for secession as the "final alternative": "You too know, that among us, white men have an equality resulting from a presence of a lower caste, which cannot exist where white men fill the position here occupied by the servile race" (Davis vol. 3). While the causes of the Civil War are far more complex than what the space in this chapter will allow me to discuss, it is important to note that the issue of slavery was a central source of the escalating political tension that would result in the South's secession. While slavery was the primary matter at hand, white southern rhetors often made use of deflection as a tactic to further sustain their power.

Rather than make race a central issue, white Southerners often couched their claims for independence and control over slaves as necessary for the preservation of their society. The argument for states' rights has long been used as a battle cry by southerners when they have felt infringed upon. During the Civil War, Confederate soldiers likened themselves to the second generation of Revolutionary War fighters and thus deflected attention from the role of slavery in their rebellion: "when Confederates cast themselves as the guardians of Revolutionary ideals, they avoided discussing other causes of the war, specifically slavery" (Rubin 86). The deflection of race as a means to support white supremacist ideology is a key characteristic of southern rhetoric that would surface again in arguments made against the implementation of *Brown*.

Historians have not been alone in their quest to investigate the ways in which southern identity invoked racialized constructions of citizenship. Patricia Roberts-Miller's *Fanatical Schemes: Proslavery Rhetoric and the Tragedy of Consensus* and Kimberly Harrison's *The Rhetoric of Rebel Women: Civil War Diaries and Confederate Persuasion* demonstrate how rhetorical practices were tied to upholding identities that profited from the preservation of white power. Roberts-Miller argues that proslavery advocates were able to exert control over public discourse and censor points of view that criticized the institution of slavery. Roberts-Miller's examination of the discourse and arguments used to advocate for and uphold slavery demonstrates the tactics used to shift blame from slave owners to abolitionists. Harrison's close reading of Confederate women's diaries provides an understanding of how they contributed to the creation and preservation of Confederate identity and culture. Her work demonstrates the ways in which these women changed their speech and writing to protect themselves and their families in the face of war.

With the loss of the Civil War there was a need to develop a new southern identity. The rhetoric of the Lost Cause, which established a victim identity for the South after it lost the war, responded to the emotional, racial, and political needs of many white Southerners; however, it offered little in the way of real solutions for how to move forward. In spite of the need to establish a new economic foundation, rebuild infrastructure, and establish morale among its (white) people, the New South did not want to lose the characteristics and traditions that made the Old South so revered, as seen in the proliferating public memorials and as pined for in shared stories passed down. Advocates for the New South "vowed to use industrial development to northernize their region's economy while doing their best to restore and uphold the most distinctively southern ideals of the Old South, especially its racial, political, and class hierarchies" (Cobb 68).

Ulrich B. Phillips, a historian whose research spanned the antebellum South and slavery, argued that, more than the South's commitment to agrarian economic institutions, it was the region's "preoccupation with race" that distinguished it from other regions (qtd. in Woodward 10). While at the dawn of the twentieth century the South was still busy trying to decide what its post-Reconstruction identity would be, the issue of race was, at least from the position of whites in power, already a decided matter. Those who pushed the issue of equality for Blacks "could be denounced as outsiders, intruders, meddlers" (Woodward 10). These were labels that would persist. While the South had to change in order to survive after the Civil War, what remained consistent were its attitudes about race.

The "Virginia Way" of Postslavery Racism

Long before Massive Resistance, politicians and civic leaders across Virginia subscribed to what the Virginia historian and segregationist Douglas Southall Freeman dubbed the "Virginia Way." This phrase described a relationship constructed with separation by consent. The white community crafted laws and social norms that secured their power, and the Black community abided by these rules because their lives often depended on it. The historian Jill Ogline Titus argues that, through the Virginia Way, whites viewed themselves as the vanguards of rights and civil liberties based on the notion that they were the guardians of the welfare of Virginia Blacks, who could manage their lives only if their rights were strictly limited. This concept directly connects to how whites imagined and practiced social control through citizenship.

In line with the Virginia Way, arguments for Massive Resistance presented a familiar paternalistic rhetoric and framed upholding segregation as whites' civic duty to protect all Virginians. The structure of these arguments relied on the projection of an ethos of care and concern for maintaining a peaceful society, on fearmongering that characterized integration as triggering an end to society, and on logic grounded in the belief that the peaceful coexistence of both Blacks and whites required segregation. Slavery and Jim Crow had institutionalized racism across the South in a way that supported legalized white control over Black lives while simultaneously never naming whiteness as a social construct that was at the root of such action. As George Lipsitz writes in *The Possessive Investment in Whiteness: How White People Profit from Identity Politics*, "[C]onscious and' deliberate actions have institutionalized group identity in the United States, not just through the dissemination of cultural stories, but also through the creation of social structures that generate economic advantages for European Americans through the possessive investment in whiteness" (2). This investment directed the leaders of the Massive Resistance movement to turn to state laws as a way of institutionalizing segregation and resistance to federal interference (Titus 14).

As with all arguments, it matters both what is said and who says it. Those who made the most public declarations for Massive Resistance in Virginia, as well as throughout the region, relied on a constructed identity that was readily accepted by their audience. This identity was carefully constructed through memorials to Civil War heroes, melodramatic public laments and nostalgia that longed-for tradition, and public histories crafted and circulated so as to maintain dominant narratives about the necessity of white control for the benefit of all of society. The arguments for sustaining segregation harkened back to those histories and arguments made both during and after the Civil War. Generally speaking, they maintained that whites needed to be in control of Black lives because Blacks were inept. Similar arguments were used to support the institution of slavery and laws developed to exercise control over Black lives during the Jim Crow era. This constructed white identity excluded Blacks from full citizenship and cast them as dependent upon whites for guidance and structure. What remains consistent about the arguments made for white control over the Black community was the ironic construction of race as being both the reason and yet *not* the reason. Some reactions from the white community to the *Brown* decision against segregation reflected this stance.

Historians generally identify three camps among southern whites in their reaction to *Brown*: segregationists who resisted integration; moderates who remained cautious about the implications of racial mixing but rejected outright defiance of the ruling; and a small number of progressives who worked as allies of the Black community (Titus 17; Newman 21; Pahowka 46). The most extreme segregationists called for the abolition of the Supreme Court, abandonment of public schools, and confinement of whites who supported integration to mental institutions (Bartley 68–69; Bonastia 49). US Senator Harry Byrd Sr., a Virginia Democrat and leading segregationist, dubbed the extreme segregationists' efforts "Massive Resistance." This movement framed decisions such as Prince Edward's closing of its public schools as both an expression of defiance against the court and a display of good citizenship. While moderates constituted a sizable presence in the South, the bellowing of segregationist rhetoric that described racial segregation as critical to maintaining a civil society silenced most of them (Lassiter and Lewis 1; Bonastia 7).[1]

In Virginia, Gov. Thomas Stanley's initial response to *Brown* described what he believed to be the necessary demeanor to respond to the ruling: "cool heads, calm, steady, and sound judgment" (qtd. in Smith 84). On May 24, 1954, he extended an invitation to five Black leaders from across the commonwealth to meet with him: Oliver Hill, NAACP attorney for the plaintiffs in *Brown*; Rev. Fleming Alexander and P. B. Young Sr., editors, respectively, of the *Roanoke Tribune* and the *Norfolk Journal and Guide*; James Woodson, president of the all-Black Virginia Teachers Association; and Dr. R. P. Daniel, president of Virginia State College, a historically Black college. There was little conversation at the meeting between the governor and his guests. He simply asked them to ignore *Brown* (Gates 31). They demurred. It is unknown whether Stanley believed he was powerful enough to demand this kind of request of five of the most powerful Black men in the state or if he saw it as a last-ditch effort to avoid more significant measures.

Five weeks later, on June 25, 1954, Stanley announced to the commonwealth through news outlets, "I shall use every legal means at my command to continue segregated schools in Virginia" (qtd. in Smith 85). That November, he created the Gray Commission, whose mandate was to study the possible effect of *Brown* on Virginia. This group failed to reach any solid conclusions, and the "Gray Plan" submitted to Stanley in November 1955 advanced no real guidelines; however, in keeping with the rhetoric of local control, the plan suggested delegating to local school boards the power of determining the placement of students. Byrd and his compatriots considered the plan too tame because it took no direct stand against *Brown*. Many segregationists feared that some counties and areas in the state, primarily those closest to Washington, DC, would decide to integrate. James Jackson Kilpatrick, editor of Richmond's main newspaper, the *News Leader*, began to publish editorials on the theory of interposition, in which states asserted a right to deem federal action unconstitutional. There was so much support for this concept among white lawmakers in the commonwealth that the Virginia General Assembly passed its Resolution on Interposition on February 1, 1956, with an overwhelming majority vote, clearly marking its defiance of the Supreme Court.

Virginia became the first state to pass a Massive Resistance policy package, in a special session of the assembly that the governor called in August 1956. These laws included creation of the Student Pupil Placement Board, which would take away local authorities' power to assign students to schools and give it to the state. The new legislation also gave the governor the power to take over any school ordered to desegregate, close it, and reopen it as a segregated school. The legislation established a tuition grant program to ensure that students could afford to pay for private "segregation academies," and it established rules that would make it difficult for the NAACP to sue districts that violated *Brown*. All of these efforts were masked under an argument that invoked the state's obligation to uphold and protect the rights of citizens as the rationale for denying Black students access to equitable educations and for thwarting integration. Virginia's political leaders set the tone for much of the South with regard to establishing arguments that subverted white supremacist ideologies as being the reason for sustaining segregation.[2]

The Southern Manifesto against *Brown*

At the national level, Senator Byrd, along with Sen. Strom Thurmond (a South Carolina Democrat until 1964 and a Republican thereafter), drafted the Southern Manifesto, or "Declaration of Constitutional Principles," in February and March 1956. Nineteen senators and eighty-two representatives from Alabama, Arkansas, Florida, Georgia, Louisiana, Mississippi, North Carolina, South Carolina, Tennessee, Texas, and Virginia signed the manifesto prior to its introduction to the Senate on March 12, 1956. The manifesto represented the first regional argument opposing integration and became the segregationists' battle cry. Echoing the South's historic arguments against federal usurpation, it used evocative language and called for vigilance against a ruling that endorsers felt was sure to destroy a way of life. The manifesto began with a description of the Supreme Court as misguided and hungry for power: "The unwarranted decision of the Supreme Court in the public-school cases [meaning *Brown*] is now bearing the fruit always produced when men substitute naked power for established law." It castigated the judges for usurping state power: "We regard the decision of the Supreme Court in the school cases as clear abuse of judicial power. The declaration climaxes a trend in the Federal judiciary undertaking to legislate, in derogation of the authority of Congress, and to encroach upon the reserved rights of the states and the people" ("Southern Manifesto"). Supporters of Massive Resistance would consistently focus on states' rights and avoid mention of race in this manner, an approach echoing the rhetoric during the Civil War and Reconstruction that focused on states' rights in lieu of addressing the issue of slavery and its atrocities.[3]

The manifesto was grounded in a logic that *Brown* violated constitutional law, and it pointed to the absence of any mention of education in the Constitution. *Brown*, according to the manifesto, was exemplary of "the Supreme Court's encroachments on rights reserved to the states and to the people, contrary to established law and to the Constitution." The signatories "commended the motives of those states which have declared the intention to resist forced integration by any lawful means." In this juxtaposition, the manifesto frames resistance as a form of good citizenship—deflecting the issue of race and highlighting their support for the Constitution. The signatories continued their appeal with a focus on garnering support from those who may not feel they had any connection to the matter: "We appeal to the states and people who are not directly affected by these decisions to consider the constitutional principles involved against the time when they too, on issues vital to them, may be the victims of judicial encroachment. . . . [W]e have full faith that a majority of the American people believe in the dual system of government which has enabled us to achieve our greatness and will in time demand that the reserved rights of the states and of the people be made secure against judicial usurpation." Thus, the manifesto appealed to a broader group of citizens, including those outside of the South. "All Americans," they contended, needed to be vigilant against misuses of power by the federal government. The manifesto concludes with the signatories' pledge "to use all lawful means to bring about a reversal of this decision" ("Southern Manifesto").

The practice of Massive Resistance flourished throughout the South. Virginia, as the onetime capital of the Confederacy, became the model for the region based on its legislative practices and leadership (Bartley 68; Gates xvii; Titus 17). Virginia's political structure, social climate, history, and constructions of race in many ways birthed the perfect rhetorical situation in which opposition to integration could thrive.

The Byrd Organization and Massive Resistance in Virginia

Historians generally view Senator Byrd as the architect of Massive Resistance in Virginia (Bartley 117; Heinemann 327). Byrd's political leadership, including his four years as governor (1926–30) and more than thirty years as a US senator (1933–65), afforded him the ability to both control and influence politics for decades. His network of supporters, often referred to as the Byrd Organization, dominated Virginia politics and forged strong relationships with politicians throughout the state. He built a reputation for strong fiscal conservatism that would also be manifested in his rhetoric supporting continued segregation. While most southern politicians shared his belief in segregation, the extensive network he held throughout Virginia secured him an audience larger than most politicians could command in their own states. The seat of his power was the Fourth District of the state, known as the Southside, an area that included Prince Edward County.

Senator Byrd's first public pronouncement on *Brown* came as a press release just hours after the ruling on May 17, 1954. Writing on a day he and many other southern whites considered catastrophic, deeming it "Black Monday," Byrd described the moment as a continuation of the South's historical struggle to wage resistance against perceived federal infringement. Employing long-standing "god terms," such as liberty, citizenship, and states' rights, he warned of complete devastation to society at the hands of integrationists.[4] These terms have traditionally been associated with white southerners' attempts to maintain laws and customs that promote segregation. These terms held weight because of the ideologies and traditions they carried with them.

His statement opened as follows: "The unanimous decision of the Supreme Court to abolish segregation in public education is not only sweeping but will bring implications and dangers of the greatest consequence. . . . Abolition of segregation will create problems such as have never confronted us before." He labeled *Brown* "the most serious blow that has yet been struck against the rights of the states in a matter vitally affecting their authority and welfare" (*Brown* Press Release). Reportedly, Byrd was outraged by Governor Stanley's initial call for "cool heads" (Heinemann 325). By defining segregation as a states' rights issue, Byrd connected it to what southern whites considered a litany of recognizable offenses against them, all perpetrated by the federal government since before the Civil War. His audience associated states' rights with the case for southern secession and the protection of the South's rights to slave labor, which made his words resonate with that group. Byrd's argument framed *Brown* as part of an ongoing attack on the southern way of life.

The press release continued by describing separate but equal schools as products of white southerners' long-standing belief that they offered "generosity" and "goodwill" to Black citizens. Byrd warned that the high court's decision would waste funds the state had allocated to construct schools for Black children: "One of cruelest results arising out of this 'about-face' of the Supreme Court is that the Southern States, accepting the validity of the previous decision in recent years, have expended hundreds of millions of dollars for construction of new Negro school facilities to conform with the policy previously laid down by the Court." Byrd's characterization of whites as benevolent benefactors of Black education would resonate with listeners who had no recognition of, or interest in, the very real discrepancies between Black and white schools in most localities. Further, Byrd cast southern whites as law-abiding victims trying to satisfy the whims of waffling courts: "Great progress has been made at tremendous cost throughout the Southern States to carry out that which our Southern State Governments had the right to believe was the law of the land." By emphasizing economic arguments, which his history of fiscal conservatism enabled, Byrd effectively directed attention and culpability away from the issue of inequality. White southerners were victimized by the federal government, he argued, and the release concluded by declaiming that *Brown* would "be deplored by millions of Americans, and, instead of promoting the education of our children . . . [would] have the opposite effect in many areas of the country" (*Brown* Press Release).

Byrd's press release on "Black Monday" was a call to arms. A letter he wrote to the Federal Commission of Education in 1958 further elucidated his rationale for opposition. His letter responded to an invitation to attend a meeting of the state's Commission on Education. At twelve pages, this letter provides a precise summary of Byrd's position and the rhetorical moves he would use repeatedly to preserve segregation. Byrd's prophecy of social devastation because the court's ruling ignored what whites had done already for Blacks would find support among sympathizers who believed that upholding separate but equal should absolve them of additional responsibilities. Like countless whites before them, leaders like Byrd presumed to know the Black community and what was best for its members. These paternalistic relationships, along with the belief that the South needed to stand up to outside meddlers (presumably northerners but really anyone who objected to the South's form of social control) gave new cause and group identity to white Virginians by calling on beliefs many already held. Writing four years after *Brown* and one year before Prince Edward's schools closed, he addressed the intervening time as well as the effects of the ruling.

The letter began with Byrd's description of *Brown* as another in a line of injudicious attacks on the rights of Virginians. The federal courts, he wrote, were using "illegal methods" to "bring Virginia to her knees"—meaning, implicitly, white Virginians. All Virginians, he claimed, shared his "unanimous" perspective, and *Brown* had therefore made them "now even more opposed to enforced integration against the nearly unanimous sentiment of the Virginia people" (Letter 1). By constructing his supporters as all inhabitants of the state, Byrd invoked the idea that white and Black southerners alike had the obligation to resist integration for the welfare of both the Black and white communities.

Byrd spends much of the letter building an argument against federal intervention: "Our schools should never be under the iron fist of the federal bureaucracy if we are to protect our posterity. Any weakening of resistance to judicial legislation would lead to the further withering away of State sovereignty as a curb against federal despotism" (Letter 1). He equated desegregation with a federal takeover of the schools and further stoked the fear of federal usurpation. Byrd believed states needed to be protected against the "federal octopus" (qtd. in Heinemann 330). Casting Virginia as the victim, Byrd argued that the courts singled out Virginia by challenging its social codes. He contended, "Never in the history of our country has any State been subjected, in time of peace, to tyrannical oppression such as Virginia has undergone in the last four years. We were the target" (Letter 2). It is important to remember that *Brown* comprised several cases from across the United States. Only one came from Virginia, but Byrd's attempt to stoke the fears of his followers involved directing their attention to what he felt was intrusion into how Virginia wanted to carry out (or ignore) the *Brown* ruling. By describing the four years since the *Brown* ruling as a period of "tyrannical oppression," Byrd connects his argument to the Civil War–era states' rights rhetoric, which, his biographer notes, was his most typical way of opposing integration (Heinemann 329).

The letter also disparages the NAACP's actions, identifying them as the impetus behind the maltreatment of Virginia: "The NAACP, in the early stages, decided on the line of battle. It decreed that Virginia should be conquered first and, in the meantime, other Southern States would not be disturbed" (Byrd, Letter 3). The senator casts the NAACP as a manipulative, law-evading group: "Let us face the facts frankly, and let no one be led to believe that we may expect moderation from the NAACP unless it is done so on a temporary basis and for motives of strategy" (Letter 5). Demonizing the public face of Black activism further supported his case for segregation itself. Byrd states his accusation: "The NAACP today, is, in fact, the fourth branch of the Government, unauthorized by Congress, it is true, and the only difference is that the NAACP lawyers are not on the public payrolls." The federal government, in this formulation, has delegitimized itself by alliance with an irresponsible, lawless group. He calls on the commission to "devise ways and means to keep us from the terrible tradition that confronts us" and "to evaluate [its course of action] from a standpoint of the relationship between the two races and social activities of our public school system." Nine years before *Loving v. Virginia*, he ties integration and the social nature of school activities to "increasing marriage between the races" (Letter 6). Given the fear of miscegenation by many whites and the accepted nature of miscegenation laws, this rhetoric would also resonate strongly with his listeners. His letter to the commission ends with a warning: "I know your Commission will surely conclude that without unrelenting and increasing resistance we cannot preserve our form of government" (Letter 7). Byrd's own district would affirm this insistence on increasing resistance to integration all in the name of practicing good citizenship. Byrd's letter reveals his reliance on Civil War–era rhetoric and the Virginia Way. In warning of the ruin of civilization because of miscegenation and by accusing the federal government of tyranny, he acknowledged the concerns of many southern whites. His paternalistic construction of their role in society appealed to them.

Byrd also directly addressed the Prince Edward County school closures in a document written sometime after the May 1959 announcement that the schools would be shuttered. Byrd opened the document with accolades for his white constituents' resistance. He praised the county residents' "fortitude . . . in fighting to preserve their rights" and applauded their "rare courage" (Untitled 2). He invoked Thomas Jefferson, saying that the county had followed his emphasis on local control of education. Thus, he framed the resistance as part of a larger American legacy. Byrd suggests the actions of the school board were a civic expression of a duty to control education, which establishes a brand of citizenship based in hierarchies and difference as a means of civil control.

Byrd glorified the white community's move to establish the private, all-white Prince Edward Academy after the closure of the county's public schools: "You stand today as a symbol of Virginia's glorious traditions. Knowing your conditions, I am convinced you have taken the only course to preserve a system of education in the County of Prince Edward" (Untitled 2). He praised the efforts of white Prince Edwardians who were creating a private school system for their children as well as their offers to "help" their Black neighbors establish a similar system, omitting to mention that the Black community had never entertained cooperating with fundraising efforts whites offered to undertake on behalf of an all-Black private school system. Byrd reaffirms references to white benevolence and innocence that he earlier attributed to all white Virginians.

In contrast to his previous warnings that *Brown* would bring violence and chaos, in this document addressing Prince Edward's school system Byrd describes peace: "I know of no other community in Virginia where relations between the white and colored population have been more harmonious and interdependent than in Prince Edward" (Untitled 3). The interdependence Byrd referred to consisted of Black people doing much of the menial work in the county for meager wages, and the harmony he described hinged on the constant threat of violence against Black people who sought to disrupt the hierarchy. It is true that Black and white communities were interdependent on one another, as was true for many rural communities; however, this perceived harmony existed largely because white communities exerted control over resources and instilled fear in those who dared to speak against the status quo. Thus, stability was contingent upon whites punishing Blacks and threatening violence during resistance to white supremacist ideology. Byrd's writing illustrates continued preservation of a rhetorical landscape that made arguments about racial categorization and citizenship status indistinguishable. Byrd's commitment to Massive Resistance was a result of fear of Black emancipation. His biographer notes that increased political participation threatened the Byrd organization. If Blacks became voters, they would likely have voted against Byrd and his allies. Byrd fought against changes to the poll tax and any legislation that would improve Black access to voting. Opposing the *Brown* decision was part of his plan to stop any and all attempts at dismantling Jim Crow and to keep the traditional power structure in place (Heinemann 330).

The Defenders of State Sovereignty and Individual Liberties

The Defenders were key responders to Byrd's call for white citizens to mobilize against the *Brown* rulings. A small group comprising prominent leaders and citizens first met in Virginia's Southside, where Byrd's support was strongest, a month after the first *Brown* ruling. Members included established community leaders such as Garland Gray, a state senator; J. Barrye Wall, publisher of the local *Farmville Herald* newspaper; and Robert Crawford, a business owner and chair of the school board, also of Prince Edward. The Defenders would grow quickly over the next year and by early 1955 would have multiple chapters throughout the state, as well as members from all levels of state and local government. They became Virginia's most influential segregationist group, and their publications influenced Virginia's Massive Resistance legislative policy package. In part, their power came from the influential positions their members held in local and state government and public spaces. Like Byrd, the Defenders argued that integration threatened the rights of all citizens in Virginia and that white citizens had an obligation to act to preserve segregation. Their name, Defenders of State Sovereignty and Individual Liberties, employed the same trigger terms Byrd used—liberty, citizenship, and states' rights—and their written platform also continued that type of rhetoric.

The Defenders circulated pamphlets, recruited members, and published editorials in newspapers throughout Virginia. They actively designed their rhetoric to harness a sympathetic audience to aid recruitment and, like Byrd, argued that the *Brown* ruling threatened to destroy their way of life by challenging states' rights. Their rhetoric deflected attention from issues of race and power as well as culpability. Their pamphlet *Principles for Which We Stand* outlines the group's mission statement and history. It opens with ten statements of principle, including three that succinctly present their vision:

> That, the Constitution establishing a Republic of the Several States of America gave certain enumerated powers to the Federal Government and expressly reserved the remainder of the powers to the several states;

> That, each state can best protect the rights and provide for the well-being of the citizens within its jurisdiction;

> That, attempts to change the lawful manner, mores, and traditions of any state of these United States of America by any branch of the Federal Government is an infringement of the sovereignty of the states composing this Union.

The principles do not include any direct reference to *Brown* or integration; instead the focus is on states' rights, which in the matter of segregation would enable whites to continue to control Blacks. The Defenders also looked for support from outside the commonwealth as they extended their argument to advocate for the right of "any state" to resist the federal government. The same pamphlet describes the group's purpose: "To instill a recognition of the worth to each individual of the historic liberties the citizens of the United States have enjoyed, and to increase the determination to defend those liberties by all honorable and lawful means against all efforts to encroach thereon." For some, an interpretation of this statement is that Black people are not citizens and that to extend to them the rights of citizenship would automatically infringe on the liberties of whites. The Defenders held that they were obligated to "preserve the powers reserved [therein] to the States and to the people" because these powers clearly meant white control (*Principles*).

Like Byrd, the Defenders figured whites as the patrons who controlled the Black community, and they invoked racial harmony as a product of segregation: "We are convinced that certain subversive forces and pressure groups are at work in our midst setting class against class and race against race in order to destroy the harmony that must prevail if we are to remain a strong and unified nation" (*Principles*). This desire for maintaining harmony was another oft-invoked theme in southern white supremacist rhetoric. While preserving segregation to create unity is ironic, the Defenders suggested that integration could ignite another civil war.

Their pamphlets garnered attention, but the Defenders document that made the strongest impression on the political landscape was issued in June 1955: "Plan for Virginia." This document outlined nine pivotal proposals for upholding segregation: (1) holding a special session of the Virginia General Assembly to amend the state's constitution; (2) amending section 129 of the state's constitution to give the assembly power to adopt laws in relation to schools; (3) granting schools funding to cover the expense of children attending private schools if public schools closed; (4) repealing laws for compulsory education; (5) proposing that the assembly enact laws to prohibit the use of state funds for integrated schools; (6) adopting laws that would make tuition grants available for private segregated schools; (7) pledging their support to enacting these proposals "to prevent the mixing of the races;" (8) having all candidates for the assembly "make known at once, with frankness and candor, what may be their position on this critical school question"; and (9) calling on all who held public office in Virginia to make known their position ("Plan for Virginia" 4). The Defenders' "Plan for Virginia" declared the exigency of the moment: "The Defenders are amazed that there be those in our midst who would lull our people into a false sense of security by assuring them that under these decisions we have all the time we want in which to chart our course. The Court has not given that time." The group called upon Virginia's leaders and citizens to react against the Supreme Court's demand for integration with "all deliberate speed": "There be those who after a year of talk still advocate that nothing now be done, but that we take our time in an endeavor to 'hammer out' some plan of procedure unknown to them and to us. We call upon such persons, and particularly any such who have been honored by election to the General Assembly, to meet their responsibility and to state in frankness and candor to the people of Virginia what they have to offer" ("Plan for Virginia" 3). In their impatience for action, the group constructed a paradigm that punished with public exposure any supporters or legislators who could have proceeded more cautiously in defying the federal government.

The Defenders predicted imminent danger from inaction: "Unless something be done, and unless something be done now, integration will begin in Virginia, and once begun, it, like every other vile pestilence, will spread to the point where it has covered the whole body politic. Whether it come in our day, our children will see the death of our Anglo-Saxon civilization" ("Plan for Virginia," 3–4). The descriptor "Anglo-Saxon" clearly marked racial lines. The Defenders understood integration as a powerful threat to the prevailing power structure. Like Byrd, they continued to frame citizenship through the preservation of a segregated system: "Those who talk of preserving our public school system know not of what they speak. Our public school system—that system which we have known for many years in Virginia, which has been so beneficial to white persons and which rescued the Negros out of illiteracy—cannot be preserved. The United States Supreme Court has killed it for years to come" (7). Like Byrd, the Defenders described Virginia's "separate but equal" system of public education as altruistic, thus fashioning whites as caring citizens, and the preservation of segregation as a means to assure the good of all. Governor Stanley called a special session of the assembly in August 1956 to pass a Massive Resistance policy package that was heavily influenced by the Defenders' principles. The policy package described earlier in this chapter had severe implications around the state and set Prince Edward on a trajectory toward school closures.

The turning point for the implementation of Virginia's Massive Resistance legislation came in September 1958. Gov. J. Lindsay Almond, only months into his term, used Massive Resistance laws to lock some thirteen thousand students out of schools in Charlottesville, Norfolk, and Warren County because of their plans to integrate. These larger districts found it impossible to create alternative school options for white students because of the sheer number of students and a lack of resources. The tables were turned when white parents in these communities found their children without schooling.[5] The courts would respond as well. The Virginia Supreme Court overturned the school closure law at the same time the federal court ruled against the closures.

Governor Almond initially pledged his support to the Massive Resistance package, and his initial efforts to close the aforementioned schools demonstrated that commitment. When the courts ruled against the closures, Almond surprisingly called not for more defiance but for a special session of the assembly, to repeal the Massive Resistance laws.[6] While Massive Resistance, as manifest in a set of legislative policies, was officially over in most of Virginia, Prince Edward County had only begun its display of allegiance to the ways of the Old South.

Closing School Prince Edward Schools with All Deliberate Speed

Prince Edward's trajectory toward Massive Resistance was different than what occurred in the rest of the state. The Prince Edward County Board of Supervisors proclaimed an emergency following the May 1955 call for "all deliberate speed" in *Brown* II. Those in power began to draft their plans for keeping school integration at bay. Public attendees encouraged officials to refuse to appropriate money for schools, and the board responded, appropriating only the minimum for building upkeep and maintenance. In keeping with Byrd's references to *Plessy v. Ferguson*'s (1896) "separate but equal" clause, county leaders argued that the building of the all-Black Moton High School was an expression of their goodwill. The board's minutes reveal that it never considered school integration. The only solution on the table was resistance.

The Defenders marshaled tremendous support for local resistance to *Brown*

Figure 2. Robert R. Moton High School, Prince Edward County, Virginia, No Trespassing sign, 1962–63. Edward H. Peeples Prince Edward County (VA) Public Schools, Virginia Commonwealth University James Branch Cabell Library. Special Collections and Archives.

in Prince Edward County. More than fifteen hundred white attendees packed every seat and the hallway at Jarman Hall on the Longwood College campus in Farmville on June 7, 1955 (Murrell 140). J. Barrye Wall presented the Defenders' plan of closing public schools should the courts order them to integrate. Other white community leaders also voiced their support, among them Louis Dahl, owner of a sporting goods store and member of the chamber of commerce, and Robert Crawford, former chair of the school board. Recognizing that the community might oppose the closure of public schools without provisions in place for their children, the meeting laid plans for a private fundraising corporation to craft what would later become the Prince Edward Academy (Bonastia 28). Crawford, Dahl, and Wall led the charge thereafter, arguing that segregation was necessary for the good of the entire community and, as Byrd and the Defenders had said in other forums, that whites had long since done enough to support Black education. They used the prestige gained from their positions in the community to secure their audience and assure them that they had the best interests of the county at heart. These men held powerful positions and were well respected. This was also political theater because, prior to the meeting, conversations took place to arrange support for calls for school closures and to organize pro-segregation speakers. There were a few local voices of dissent: Longwood professors Foster Greshman and Henry Bittinger; James Bash, the principal of the all-white Farmville High School; and the Reverend James Kennedy, a Presbyterian minister. Their small number and more progressive ideas meant that their objections had little effect in a closed community that was run by a select few.

Bittinger spoke against the move to close schools in the Jarman Hall meeting and was active with the American Friends Service Committee. Additionally, James Bash spoke against the creation of a private school system. He was particularly vocal in the Jarman Hall meeting about the problems he believed would surface with a move to private schooling, such as lower staff salaries and the loss of state retirement benefits. Bash would ultimately tell the crowd "that his public-school loyalties would prevent him from ever accepting a check from a private corporation formed to evade a Supreme Court ruling" (Titus 29). The Reverend James Kennedy, pastor of Farmville's Presbyterian congregation, voiced his opposition in the meeting along with Gresham. Both offered an alternative to guarantee the salaries of all the teachers (both Black and white) who would go without income because of the closures. Kennedy cited his Christian faith to explain his support for exploring alternatives to the closures. He said they would cause dissension at his church and that he would end up having to leave because his congregation did not like his stance.

An additional prominent local voice opposed to the school closures was that of another Longwood College faculty member, Dr. C. G. G. Moss. He was a professor of American history and also served as an academic dean. For Dr. Moss, his academic commitment to teaching also had an activist component: "I've been teaching American history for forty years. I've been teaching that democracy and social justice are the greatest ideas of the American nation. I'd be a traitor to the thousands of students I've taught if I didn't take a stand for these ideals when the opportunity comes" (qtd. Titus 106–7). In spite of any early reservations Moss displayed toward integration, he radically changed his perspective and became "the county's most outspoken white dissenter" (Titus 106). Moss wrote letters to the editor of the *Farmville Herald*, spoke out at budget hearings for the school board, and sought opportunities to speak directly with leaders in the Black community. He would make the ultimate statement of support for integration by sending his seventeen-year-old son, Dickie, to the Free School.

In addition to these dissenters, there was another fringe group known as the Bush League, a name coined after the fact that they often met in the bushes or in the far reaches of the county to avoid being seen. Members of the Bush League didn't want to be called integrationists, but they were against the school closures. They were not altruistic about educating all students in Prince Edward, however; their primary concern was the county's economy: "They were businessmen, by and large, not unlike similar groups that worked to reopen schools briefly closed by the Almond administration elsewhere in the state" (Smith 179). Like other dissenters, the group found that their argument gained no traction and was little recognized, partially because Prince Edward was a segregationist stronghold. Given the social and economic makeup of Prince Edward at the time, and the power in numbers and authority held by the proponents of segregation, it is not difficult to see how this minority found it impossible to stop the school closures. They were marked as outsiders, and in a small southern community like Prince Edward, that kind of mark meant certain social death.

The Jarman Hall meeting propelled the segregationist cause further. A July 1955 announcement from a special three-judge district court panel that the county needed to begin to make preparations to desegregate prompted little concern, as no specific date for the charge was given; however, in response the board of supervisors adopted a "heretofore" policy in which they appropriated school budgets for only thirty days at a time. School would open for the 1955–56 academic year, and the special private school corporation kept the funds they'd raised as backup. At a school board meeting in May 1956, public attendees stood to express approval when the board decided to continue their "heretofore" approach to budgetary considerations. Additionally, a document presented at the meeting contained more than four thousand signatures from whites pledging to abandon public schooling should schools be forced to integrate. The document exemplified the same rhetorical tactics Byrd and others had presented, avoiding mention of race and blaming the "tyrannical" federal government for making the closures necessary.

Fourth District Court judge Sterling Hutcheson ruled that conditions in Prince Edward necessitated a delay in compliance with *Brown* until the start of the 1965 school year. Hutcheson's rationale was based on his belief that the community would need more time to adjust. The repeal of Virginia's Massive Resistance legislation in January 1959 left Prince Edward's resistance without the protection of state statutes. The Fourth Circuit Court of Appeals reversed Hutcheson's ruling on May 5, 1959, and ordered the county to take steps to enroll Black students in its public schools, not in 1965 but in September 1960. True to its words of warning, Prince Edward was quick to respond.

At the end of the 1958–59 school year the Prince Edward County Board of Supervisors rejected the budget submitted by the school board. Supervisors adopted a budget that allocated no money for schools and reduced property taxes by 53 percent (Bonastia 100). With this move, public schools were effectively closed in Prince Edward. Board members encouraged residents to use the money that would have gone to taxes to support the private school system (Titus 31). As described in chapter 1, the school board expressed in the *Farmville Herald* its "fervent hope" that public schools would resume "upon a basis acceptable to all," implying that only the right to continue segregation would make public education possible (Smith 151). Prince Edward clearly marked how far its leadership would go to uphold segregation. Yet, in spite of the white community's best efforts to monopolize the conversation about who had the right to define what was acceptable, the Black community would not be silenced.

Prayer, Pushing, and a Petition from the Black Community

Prince Edward County's Black community developed a variety of responses to the school closure rhetoric that permeated the area. Some Black families moved outright, while others would wake in the early predawn hours to transport their children across county lines to localities with functioning schools. The NAACP pursued a legal solution to reopen the schools through court order, but the courts moved slowly. All of the responses from the Black community reveal that their sole focus was caring for their community, expressing their hope in integration, and seeking recognition as full citizens.

One of the primary sites that influenced action and this counterresponse was the Black church.[7] Historically, the Black church has been an institution in which Blacks had space and agency that were not directly under the watch or influence of whites. The institutional roots go back to the slavery era, when slaves often gathered to worship in cabins, woods, or ravines to get as far away as possible from the danger of being found gathered together in a prohibited assembly. These meetings served not only as places for spiritual uplift but as sites to plan for liberation and resistance. Slaves would often share information about pending revolts or escape plans. While it is true that some masters allowed slaves to gather for worship, these were spaces where the white masters were normally in control of the messages. The hush harbors, or slave gatherings, that went undetected are the roots of the modern Black church (Raboteau 333). As Shirley Wilson Logan has noted, these places "also enabled the development of rhetorical abilities, including catechetical instruction, preaching, praying, and singing songs of worship with lyrics that often served the political purpose of communicating plans of escape" (12). From these spaces and contexts—from the dire need for a space to sustain the Black community's quest for liberation—the Black church was born.

Keith Gilyard writes that the Black church has traditionally been the "primary channel by which millions of Blacks came to comprehend and speculate about the social world of which they were part" (4). Dwight Hopkins, a scholar of Black liberation theology, describes the function of the Black church in a way that resonates with Gilyard's claim: "we find Black churches and related forms of faith institutions operating on the spiritual, economic, political, and cultural levels" (1). More than a space for Sunday morning worship in the Black community, the Black church has provided crucial means of support and healing for a community subject to the abuses of racism. Likewise, in her study of the role of nonviolence and the Black church in the civil rights movement, Allison Calhoun-Brown writes that "from slavery through the long racially segregated history of the United States, when African Americans were prevented from building institutions of their own and precluded from participating in the institutions of mainstream America, churches developed and contained civil society for them. In church, one could find politics, arts, music, education, economic development, social services, civil associations, leadership opportunities, and business enterprises" (169).

The church served as the primary institutional infrastructure for the civil rights movement because it offered a space where Blacks and their allies could both mobilize and function with autonomy. The intensity of Black churches' involvement in the civil rights movement fell along a wide spectrum: "understanding that Black churches fostered development of an oppositional civic culture is also useful for understanding different levels of engagements by individual churches during the movement." While most Black churches participated in civic culture to some extent, how they went about doing so varied greatly, and "congregational-specific characteristics such as socioeconomic background, educational achievement, age composition, ministerial disposition, and theological orientation were undoubtedly important determinants of the balance" (Calhoun-Brown 173, 174). The church was able to offer the infrastructure that any social justice movement needed to be organized, but it also provided a theological grounding for why this quest for social justice was necessary. Preachers were able to tap into oppositional consciousness by referencing Bible stories about God working for the oppressed.

One particular response from within the Black church that provided critical theological and physical support for the civil rights movement came from Black liberation theology. James Cone, one of the most prolific advancers of Black liberation theology, wrote from a space demonstrating how scripture spoke to the experiences of oppressed communities. This theological movement centered on the experience of Blacks: "Black theology was born in the context of the Black community as Black people were attempting to make sense out of their struggle for freedom" (Cone, "Black Theology" 150). In the view of Cone and others, Black theologians had to come to terms with whether "rejecting Black power also meant that the Black church would ignore its political responsibility to empower Black people in their present struggle" (148). Cone wrote, "[T]he task of Black theology, then, is to analyze the nature of the gospel of Jesus Christ in the light of oppressed Blacks so they will see the gospel as inseparable from their humiliated condition, and as bestowing on them the necessary power to break the chains of oppression" (Cone, *God* 5). Not all Black preachers were influenced by this particular way of thinking, but it did influence Prince Edward's most influential Black leader, Rev. L. Francis Griffin.

Reverend Griffin, pastor of First Baptist Church of Farmville, was the most recognized voice of the Black church in Prince Edward in 1955. Described by his congregation as the "fighting preacher" and the "Prophet of Prince Edward," he commanded a great deal of respect in Prince Edward ("1,200 Attend Funeral"). After serving in the US Army and studying at Shaw University, Griffin took over the same pulpit his father had held. Espousing a commitment to Black liberation equality long before the schools closed, his sermons stirred congregants to consider what he felt was a well-defined connection between Christianity and social justice. Reverend Griffin found favor with many; the youth in particular found him to be personable and caring. His role as president of the NAACP's Virginia State Conference of Branches in 1962, in addition to his being a full-time minister, meant that Griffin's work was never done. He was also a parent. He and his wife, Adelaide, had five children affected by the school closures. While his sermons and papers remain in the hands of his family, his public arguments against the school closures display how his devotion to civil rights was intertwined with his faith. For Griffin, it was faith that would help him to express and demonstrate a commitment to sustain the community in some of its darkest hours. His promise to avoid violence markedly shaped the efforts of the Black community and reflected the spiritual dimension that grounded resistance practices for many Blacks.

Griffin's faith influenced his expressions and provided steady resolve. Martin Luther King Jr. was an influence on Reverend Griffin and helped shape the efforts undertaken by Prince Edward's Black community. As he himself often said to his congregants, "Doing something to someone is not going to help" (qtd. in Titus 47). An August 1959 article in the *Richmond Afro-American* headlined "Prince Edward Residents Seek Solution to School Problems" quoted Griffin as follows: "We believe that all problems can be solved within the framework of the Christian doctrine, without hatred, malice or ill will being shown against any people[;] we shall dedicate ourselves to the practice of constructive goodwill" (Wells). Griffin often called for communal prayer, asking for people to pray at noon on a specified day for a resolution of the school closures crisis. His reliance on a faith-based approach and pointed response displayed confidence and assuredness in the face of hatred. For Griffin, this meant taking a stance against the oppression in Prince Edward.

While Griffin was the most recognizable of the ministers in Prince Edward County, other clergy members from across the local Black church community sought to work together during this time. The Farmville Ministerial Alliance, comprising ten Black ministers from the Black Baptist and African Methodist Episcopal (AME) churches in the community, published a collective resolution against the closures. Reverends Hill, Agnew, Hendricks, Cosby, Singleton, Gamble, Dunlap, Williams, and Bass included their names alongside that of Griffin. The alliance's collective resolution was published in the *Richmond Afro-American* on June 27, 1959, in an article headlined "School Fund Slash Denounced by Prince Edward Clergymen." This article, one of the first published responses to include a Black perspective on the closures, addressed multiple audiences: the Black community, segregationists, white moderates, and potential allies. The alliance's resolution employed a structure similar to the board of supervisors' resolution closing the school, focusing on the importance of democracy and being responsible citizens. Stylistically, the alliance members' use of the pronoun "we" conveyed a united front and their fortitude. The clergy members' decision to use a structure that mirrored that of the board's resolution reveals their decision to adopt and subvert the language and rhetorical strategies those in power used to meet their needs. The alliance's use of the same rhetorical conventions as the county's board also articulated the social equality of Black leaders to that of the white leaders of the segregation proponents, thus challenging myths about Black literacy levels and lack of interest in education among members of the Black community.

The ministerial alliance's resolution opens by connecting American democracy to Christian principles and a commitment to justice: "We believe [the closure of the schools] is contrary to the simple laws of decency, the American ideal of democracy, the Christian concept of justice, and moral law of God" ("School Fund"). Thus, the testimony displayed the patriotism of Blacks and their commitment as engaged and committed Christian citizens, especially in the South.

White segregationists had described patriotism as an allegiance to America's values and traditions; here the Black community claims decency, democracy, and Christianity as the impetus for integration. Building on the public faith-talk that was important for their Black and white audiences, the ministers unpacked their argument as being both about maintaining their civic duties and arguing for a form of Christianity that was not tied to racial subjugation.[8]

The repeated use of the pronoun "we" in the statement also suggests that the ministers were taking on the role of being representatives of the Black community. Gwendolyn Pough describes the function of the representative role in the Black community and posits that those who act as representatives "have access to a public voice." In this role, many use the position "to correct wrongs and replace stereotyped representation of Blacks in the United States with more positive images." Pough further explores the difficulty such a role involves, as there is no one person who can speak for all members of a group; however, "systemic regulation and exclusion force the minority to go to great lengths to claim public space—even if it means becoming a representative" (22). This representative role was often complicated by the need for the speaker to also maintain a level of respectability for white audiences, an often difficult task since respectability itself is subjective. The collective voice of these ministers functioned in this way, as they brought to the forefront their beliefs in both the importance of education and obedience to laws, two attitudes that segregationists did not ascribe to Blacks. With a collective voice, the ministers responded to the segregationists' claims about the Black community and encouraged its members to hold on to hope.

Many whites were simply ignorant of the beliefs of the Black community. Beyond faith in religion, the alliance's resolution expresses trust in both the Supreme Court and the NAACP: "We reaffirm our confidence and support in the Supreme Court of the United States and the National Association for the Advancement of Colored People for their unrelenting struggle to assure basic Constitutional rights to every citizen regardless of race, creed, color, or national origin" ("School Fund"). Whereas Byrd's speeches often slandered the NAACP as a shadowy arm of federal intrusion, the alliance's resolution highlighted the civil rights organization as an advocacy group desiring equality.

The ministerial alliance concluded the resolution by expressing an understanding of the implications of the school closures for the entire community: "The resolution above has been made with keen awareness of the serious jeopardy that this unwarranted action by the Prince Edward Board of Supervisors imposes upon the economy of this County and the jaundiced opinion of world sentiment that will settle on this State and nation" ("School Fund"). While the acknowledgment of the baselessness of the closures and warning about the perception others would have may not have persuaded the county to change direction, it did demonstrate an astute awareness of the importance of drawing attention to the matter as a means of obtaining allies and speaking directly to segregationists. The alliance's resolution reaffirmed commitments and beliefs the Black community had long held and sought to provide an explanation for its stance and a direct response to whites in Prince Edward. The resolution set the terms that would long guide the responses and actions of the Black community. Presenting a unified front was integral in the face of a system that held so much power to control the community. While responses to the resolution are not recorded, the actions that would arise from the Black community's faith organizations demonstrate that these were not empty words.

The Prince Edward County Christian Association

The signers of the Farmville Ministerial Alliance's resolution responded to the school closures with action as well as rhetoric. All were members of the Prince Edward County Christian Association (PECCA), a group that included both parents and ministers and seems to have formed after the closures. The group would select Griffin as president and Rev. A. I. Dunlap of Beulah AME Church as vice president. A PECCA report dated May 9, 1960, outlines the mission of the group and its platform for countering claims made in support of the closures. PECCA was careful to emphasize its intent to organize with other groups. It also underscored the importance of religion in its efforts. As an openly Christian organization, PECCA could draw on the Black churches' influence in the Black community. It also framed its goals in terms of citizenship: "This association is governed by a constitution which is rigid in its objectives, but elastic enough to permit us to deal with all of the problems that now hamper our complete acceptance as first-class citizens" (PECCA 4). The report describes the relationship between being a Christian and being an active democratic citizen as natural and harmonious: "We believe that under the determined Christian and democratic leadership of this organization, the citizens of Prince Edward County will move steadily toward a lasting and just solution to this present problem. However, we humbly recognize that all of our efforts, regardless of our determination, will fall short of our stated objectives unless we receive from outside sources strong, fortifying support" (PECCA 4).This statement expressed a commitment to social justice through Christian principles that would ultimately lead to PECCA's attainment of powerful support and alliances with the Quaker-affiliated American Friends Service Committee (AFSC).

Much to the chagrin of many in Prince Edward's white community, the AFSC, based in Philadelphia, Pennsylvania, provided considerable assistance to PECCA, including office space and equipment, as well as facilitating, as needed, teaching and curriculum support for PECCA's training centers. Established in 1917 to give young conscientious objectors ways to serve without joining the military, the AFSC had by the 1950s a long history of working for social justice ("Opening Closed Doors"). AFSC members aimed to support the local community, both Black and white residents, through the period of the school closures. Their intention was to focus on healing and reconciliation in the county, but supporting the Black community soon became its primary means for doing so. Jean Fairfax, director of southern civil rights programs for the organization, was an instrumental member of AFSC. One of the primary leaders of the AFSC's civil rights efforts both nationally and in Prince Edward, Fairfax was a Black woman from the North with degrees from Union Theological Seminary and the University of Michigan. She took an early interest in Prince Edward County's plight and would be influential in the community through both her grassroots efforts to support the needs of youth and community organizers as well as her intercession with the federal government. Her efforts would prove valuable for raising recognition and alarm with the federal government in a way that would serve as the necessary bridge between the Black community and federal leaders. This recognition made the creation of the Free School possible.

PECCA's report described the "deep scars" the Virginia Way had inflicted on the Black community: "Negro parents, having been conditioned by the innumerable overt and subtle practices of racial discrimination, found themselves at the mid-century mark frustrated and in a position bordering on utter despair" (PECCA 2). It outlines the efforts of the white community to perpetuate segregation. The report also claims that the closure of the schools threatened both Black and white children with "educational malnutrition" (3).

The report, like the alliance's resolution, reaffirmed the importance of public education in a democracy: "We realize that in a representative democracy such as ours, our governmental processes will become stagnant unless the education of citizens is broad enough to encourage maximum interest and participation according to one's ability without being hampered by artificial barriers and restrictions" (PECCA 3). With a full context and history in place for how the closures affected both Black and white children, the report built the ethos of the Black community through acknowledgment of their imperfections: "As Negro citizens of Prince Edward County, we recognize our shortcomings. We, who constitute roughly 43% of the total population, unequivocally declare that our political and civic shortcomings are many" (3). PECCA did not claim the role of hero, but it also eschewed the role of victim: "We have elected not to spend these precious days at the 'wailing wall'" (3). This move to declare their desire to do more than pray reflected Black theology's mission to match faith with works. PECCA's focus was to promote a nonviolent Christian response that placed the needs of the children first.

In addition to issuing the report, PECCA responded to the closures with three types of action. They engineered a voter registration drive, set up a program to place older students who were nearing completion of high school in programs that would let them obtain a diploma, and worked with allies from the AFSC to organize training centers designed for socialization and refreshing student skills. They declined offers from segregationists who wanted to provide funding for private Black academies. Student placement efforts and training centers tested segregationists' arguments that Blacks were not serious about education and demonstrated that the community was not dependent on handouts from Prince Edward's whites to accomplish their goals.

PECCA's training centers, housed in church basements across the county, aimed to build morale in the Black community, socialize children, and provide instruction in math and reading. They explicitly sought not to provide any program that would appear to be modeled after a full K–12 school, out of a concern that this would appear to whites as Blacks submitting to segregated schools (Tillerson-Brown 3).[9] PECCA received support from the Virginia Teachers Association (VTA), a group of Black educators who also sought to be of service to the children of Prince Edward. During the summer of 1961 they carried out a monthlong crash program to focus on reading, writing, and math skills. The school board offered to allow the use of the public school buildings for these courses, but PECCA refused this with the rationale that it did not want the program to resemble a traditional K–12 institution.

These centers demonstrated that the Black community was capable of quickly organizing in support of its children. Helen Estes Baker, resident program director for the AFSC in Prince Edward, worked to help train PECCA teachers. Baker, herself a Virginia native, developed a leadership institute to give center leaders an opportunity to discuss curriculum and citizenship and to listen to talks given about a variety of topics that they could in turn bring back to the centers and use in their work with the students. Baker served in several roles during her time in the county. In October 1960, she served as the first Prince Edward County community relations director. In this role, she helped organize the student placement program for high school students. This program would place students nearing graduation with host families living outside of the county. Baker was also expected to help foster cross-cultural communication between the Black and white communities. This proved to be the most difficult task.

Mothers in the Movement

Black women played a central role in efforts to respond to the school closures and to create a support structure that would allow the children of Prince Edward to continue their education. Narratives of the civil rights movement traditionally do not explore the role of women (Crawford, Rouse, and Woods xvii). However, scholars like Jacqueline Bacon make the contributions of women plain: "[T]hrough their devotion to education, self-help, and religions, in particular, African American women were able to voice their concerns and to assume responsibilities . . . outside the home" (Bacon, *Humblest* 49). Both the women from Prince Edward and those who, like Baker and Fairfax, came to the county did just this.

As will be shown in chapter 4, in the home, mothers often taught their children as best they could from what they knew. It was also the case that some of the women in the county had served as teachers in the public schools and, now out of work, served a vital role in continuing to educate the children. Amy Tillerson-Brown describes the network of Black women, most of them residents of the county, who worked independently of PECCA and the AFSC to facilitate educational opportunities for students. This network of homeschools, which Tillerson-Brown calls "grassroots school," were found across the county (1). These women "made public their desires to provide academic training for the community children who attended," and further, the women "who helped to organize and taught in these schools networked to sustain, and re-define their communities despite oppression" (2). One such school, run by Flossie Hudson in her home, operated from 1959 until the Free School opened. On average, she had fifty students every day during that time, and she often enlisted older children to help her run lesson plans. As in the case of the training centers, some Blacks worried that establishing anything that resembled a traditional school would hinder their case for integration and would serve as an indication that they were settling. Hudson, however, did not "mask the fact that their students were receiving academic training in her school" (Tillerson-Brown 4). The work of these women, as well as that of Helen Estes Baker and Jean Fairfax, was integral to the community. As will be discussed in the following chapter, it would be Fairfax's petitioning and consistent back and forth with the federal government that would help to open the door for Griffin and others to meet with federal stakeholders and begin work toward the Free School.

White Allies in Prince Edward

While much of the aid and assistance for the Black community came directly from within the community's own network, assistance also came from white allies outside of the county. In addition to the AFSC, which employed both whites and Blacks, as well as those local progressives who dared to voice their opposition, Edward Peeples would provide aid through scholarship, photographic documentation, and play. In January 1961, Edward Peeples, a young, white social services worker from Richmond with a newfound commitment to civil rights, heard Helen Estes Baker speak at the Richmond Council on Human Relations. He organized a baseball club for Prince Edward's teenage boys, an action that gained the notice of local police. As Peeples recalls, "Shortly after we arrived, two police cars pulled up and parked on the bluff above the playing field. Two white policemen emerged and assumed a posture to intimidate: resting the heels of their hands on their service revolvers as they swaggered back and forth, leering at our every move" (90). At the end of the game, the police officers followed Peeples and the other volunteers to the county line to show their displeasure. Nonetheless, Peeples offered recreation activities to the Black children of Prince Edward throughout the period of the school closures.[10]

Peeples's work did not stop with the baseball field. He also joined with Richmond's First Unitarian Church to organize the Richmond Committee of Volunteers to Prince Edward in July 1961. Once more working with Baker, the group used Prince Edward County's recreation center each Saturday for arts, crafts, movies, games, poetry readings, and dance classes (Titus 61). The committee comprised individuals from across ethnic backgrounds, social classes, religions, and political affiliations. Peeples's master's thesis, "A Perspective on the Prince Edward County School Issue," investigated the disparity between the Black and white communities with regard to schools. From this fieldwork, he produced several documents, some of which were later incorporated into reports and briefings for the US Commission on Civil Rights, the Department of Justice, and the Office of Education in their efforts to find a resolution to the school closures. Peeples also took photographs of school buildings throughout the county to document the discrepancies between white and Black schools. These photographs, now available through the Virginia Commonwealth University Libraries Digital Collections, give an increased level of evidence for the marked differences between the separate but supposedly equal schools.

In addition to allies like Peeples and the American Friends Service Committee, Queens College of New York sent students to provide free tutoring services during the summer of 1963.

Prince Edward Protests and Sit-Ins in Summer '63

From 1959, when the schools closed, to 1963, Prince Edward saw little violence. Nationally, the civil rights movement reached one of its most violent climaxes in 1963. Medgar Evers was killed on June 12. Fire hoses and dogs were turned on demonstrators in Birmingham, Alabama, and in Danville, Virginia, in the spring of that year. Still, at the beginning of the summer of 1963, the belief that direct action was now a necessary component of the strategy for integration was not an easy decision. As mentioned previously, sit-ins and marches had been missing from Prince Edward. The nonviolent rhetoric and direction

Figure 3. Protesters at Grants/Safeway, Farmville, Virginia, August 1963, #028. Farmville 1963 Civil Rights Protests, Virginia Commonwealth University James Branch Cabell Library. Special Collections and Archives.

of Reverend Griffin had perhaps kept Prince Edward peaceful. Historians have interpreted the lack of direct action in the county as originating from a convergence of several causes. First, the Black community and its allies did not want to detract from the work being done in the courts. Second, Prince Edward's rural location meant that organizing boycotts of white-owned stores, as protesters did in cities, would not be an easy task. The nearest alternatives for commerce were some fifty miles to the west, in Lynchburg, and sixty miles to the east, in Richmond. Finally, as in other places around the South, Prince Edward's Black community also feared retaliation by their white employers should they boycott (Titus 121; Bonastia 128).

In the summer of 1963, however, Black leaders decided protest was necessary. Griffin and Rev. Goodwin Douglass from the AME church spearheaded efforts for protests to occur in downtown Farmville with the involvement of the NAACP Youth Council. In preparation, the Student Nonviolent Coordinating Committee (SNCC) organized workshops on peaceful protests. The ensuing demonstrations opposed the school closures, discriminatory hiring practices, and economic inequality. The youth from the county made it their first mission to march on Main Street on July 25, 1963, and that march would conclude with a sit-in at the area's

Figure 4. Protesters on Main Street, Farmville, Virginia, July 1963, #015. Farmville 1963 Civil Rights Protests, Virginia Commonwealth University James Branch Cabell Library. Special Collections and Archives.

shopping center. The next day, sit-ins at the College Shoppe restaurant and State Theatre would challenge the segregation of the community's public spaces. The direct action culminated on Sunday, July 28, with demonstrators attempting "kneel-ins" at white churches. Protests would last most of the summer and utilized a variety of strategies. Some days protesters sat in at segregated lunch counters; other days they marched along main streets to block traffic.

The white community took note. An editorial in the *Farmville Herald* on August 6, 1963, headlined "Unwarranted Attack" lamented that the county had been "invaded" by people from other sections of the country: "Walking our streets with placards were youngsters, whose parents had refused to provide education for them, or who were stimulated by outside organizations to march against the people of their hometown." Once more, the Black community was made the villain and held responsible for closing schools and disrupting the community.

While young people marched in Farmville, Griffin and Fairfax took their pleas to the halls of the White House. Griffin and Fairfax presented President Kennedy with a petition signed by 650 Black Prince Edwardians (Smith 237). The petition to Kennedy asked for "a comprehensive remedial program to assist the children in transition back to school, with a specially designed hook to attract the older youth" (qtd. in Titus 138). The petition candidly called for intervention:

"The time has come for the government of the United States to insure the damage suffered by 1,700 children who have gone without formal education" ("Plan to Ask Cram Course"). The petition also put the Prince Edward struggle within a global context: "We know that our country has sent specialists to distant lands to help distressed people. . . . The children of Prince Edward County need a program which will match in purpose, scope, and quality the best social and technical assistance project which our government has ever done anywhere in the world" (qtd in Titus 138). Drawing these connections between global quests for freedom and education at home was powerful. Sen. Robert F. Kennedy had noted in an address at the Emancipation Proclamation Centennial celebration in Louisville, Kentucky, on March 18, 1963, "We may observe with as much sadness as irony that outside of the south of the Sahara[,] where education is still a difficult challenge, the only places on earth known not to provide free public education are Communist China, North Vietnam, Sarawak, Singapore, British Honduras— and Prince Edward County, Virginia" (qtd. in Lee 151). The civil rights movement was being broadcast to the world, and the irony did not escape many that as America fought to bring democracy to various parts of the world, it had work to tend to at home. White resistance to *Brown* was grounded in pleas for protection of segregation as a necessary system for civil society. These arguments were predicated upon long-standing claims by those in power that the white community knew what was best for all. This colonialist mind-set was challenged by the Black community, which responded in the courts, through the Black church, and with direct action. The Black community's three-prong approach sought to provide immediate aid to those suffering as a result of the closures, as well as long-term solutions to the conditions prompting resistance. The collaboration between the federal government, Black Prince Edwardians, leaders from the white community (at both the local and state levels), and allies like Fairfax would take careful mediation. The end result would mean free, integrated schooling for the 1963–64 school year. The next chapter describes the rhetoric that organizers crafted to support the Free School, as well as the importance of literacy in building arguments that challenged the rhetorics of Massive Resistance.

3

"Teaching Must Be Our Way of Demonstrating!"

Institutional Design against White Supremacy

The experience gained from documenting our philosophy will prove of lasting value to all of you personally and to all children attending the Free Schools.

NEIL SULLIVAN, *BOUND FOR FREEDOM*

The analysis of segregationist rhetoric in the previous chapter confirms that Massive Resistance continued to garner support in Prince Edward County despite waning as a movement across the South by the late 1950s. The Black community in Prince Edward responded to white resistance to integration through the courts, the church, demonstrations, and direct petitioning to President Kennedy for intervention. Undoubtedly, Kennedy's efforts to respond were part of a convergence of national and international events. The year 1963 was a turning point of sorts for the civil rights movement as violence steadily increased across the country. On April 12, Dr. Martin Luther King Jr. was arrested in Birmingham and would soon write his "Letter from a Birmingham Jail." The summer began with the murder of civil rights activist Medgar Evers on June 12. The Birmingham Campaign launched a series of lunch counter sit-ins, marches, and boycotts that were met with fire hoses and police dogs. King would deliver his "I Have a Dream Speech" in Washington on August 28. The press would also give more coverage to Prince Edward County, with international coverage of the demonstrations and sit-ins by Black Prince Edwardians during June and July 1963. All of these factors put pressure on Kennedy to move toward action to aid the sixteen hundred children and young people who were without schooling.

In this chapter I present and analyze arguments made during the Free School's inception and planning process, as well as the Free School curriculum itself. I begin with a description of the Free School as it moved from concept to reality. Next, I analyze the central documents (handbooks, statement of philosophy, accreditation materials, and curricular guides) that expressed the Free School's vision, mission, and curriculum. In this analysis, I demonstrate how Free School teachers and administrators responded to the ideologies of those who believed that integrated schooling was anathema to civil society; by developing curricula and pedagogical practices that acknowledged the epistemologies of their students, Free School teachers countered the arguments and actions of Massive Resistance. The overarching mission to teach students to be citizens who could "think and observe carefully" and "formulate answers that are important to our civilization" took constant negotiation among administrators, teachers, and students as they worked to construct and enact this aim as a real possibility (Sullivan, "Prince Edward County Free School Association" [Handbook] 3). This chapter's analysis illustrates the complexity involved in articulating a multifaceted institutional response to the brand of white supremacist ideology that permeated Prince Edward County.

Federal Government Intervention in Prince Edward

Once the petition circulated by local Black Prince Edwardians reached President Kennedy's desk, Jean Fairfax arranged a meeting with key federal, state, and local stakeholders. Fairfax, who had been in the county since the schools first closed, was instrumental to the process of organizing and connecting the local community with federal leaders. Burke Marshall, assistant to Atty. Gen. Robert F. Kennedy and head of the Civil Rights Division at the US Department of Justice, along with William vanden Heuvel, former diplomat and special assistant to the attorney general, represented the federal government at this meeting in late May 1963. While there were a number of allied organizations in attendance, Prince Edward attendees of note included Reverend Griffin and C. G. Gordon Moss.[1] The group's early brainstorming session resulted in several suggestions for temporary schooling in the county. There was no precedent for Prince Edward's circumstances. Recommendations ranged from broadcasting school lessons via satellite from North Carolina to the creation of federal schools on military bases. These early suggestions were not feasible; however, the meeting marked the beginning of an important series of conversations.

While conversations about scope and feasibility took place in Washington, the summer of 1963 also saw a Department of Health, Education, and Welfare (HEW)–funded research team from the Michigan State University (MSU) School of Education travel to Prince Edward to assess the damage done to the children by lack of schooling. Results of the survey, directed by Dr. Robert Green, an MSU professor of education, documented what many already knew: while a fraction of Black students had been relocated outside the county to continue their educations, the vast majority remained in Prince Edward without any access to formal education. Literacy levels were lowest among those who had never attended school (Green). The survey data, combined with vanden Heuvel's own firsthand observations from a trip to Prince Edward, confirmed what Fairfax and Griffin tried to share with anyone at the federal level who would listen: tensions were high in the community, Black children were bearing the brunt of this hardship, and something had to be done.

At a follow-up meeting in July, vanden Heuvel presented federal and community stakeholders with three possibilities based on the data collected from MSU's report and his own observations. First, private grants could be allocated to the Prince Edward School Board to operate public schools. Griffin and Moss quickly countered this option, arguing that the board could not be trusted because they were involved in the scheme that closed the schools. The second option, the use of state tuition grants, was rejected because it mirrored the financial strategy of segregation academies. The concept for a free temporary school system was conceived from the third possibility. The Free School would be open to both Black and white children, funded by private sources, and operated by its own board. Vanden Heuvel agreed to chair the school's fundraising activities. While it was unclear how many, if any, white children would enroll, the Free School marked a real possibility for integration to finally make its way to Prince Edward, something that Griffin had pressed as the only viable solution. There was general acceptance for the plan at this level, but the job of convincing Virginia's white state and local leaders remained a challenge. Meetings about the development of the school system between Griffin, Gov. Albertis Harrison's staff, Prince Edward County government officials, Virginia's NAACP representatives, and vanden Heuvel were strained. Emotions ran so high that participants were often kept in separate rooms, with vanden Heuvel serving as intermediary. In spite of the difficulties, federal stakeholders believed it necessary to establish a relationship with state and county leaders to quell concerns that the control of the school was falling into the hands of the federal government. The Free School would need to move quickly, securing infrastructure (buildings and buses), teachers, and students, to make the abbreviated implementation timeline a possibility.

Prompted by a direct request from President Kennedy, Governor Harrison assembled a six-member integrated board of trustees. Harrison, who had served as the state's attorney general before his tenure as governor, was an ally of Byrd, and his term as attorney general coincided with the state's first battles over integration. Given the roles he held, Harrison brought the knowledge and experience necessary for the establishment and development of a board for the Free School. The board's primary tasks included hiring a superintendent and conducting fundraising efforts. Board members included a former governor and presidents of Virginia's leading institutions for postsecondary education: Colgate W. Darden, former governor of Virginia and president of the University of Virginia; Dr. Fred B. Cole, president of Washington and Lee University; Dr. Robert P. Daniel, president of Virginia State University; Dr. Thomas Henderson, president of Virginia Union University, Dr. F. D. G. Ribble, former dean of the University of Virginia's law school; and Dr. Earl H. McClenney, president of St. Paul College. Drs. McClenney, Daniel, and Henderson represented three of Virginia's leading HBCUs. The board also had a fair amount of political and social clout, which provided the schools with some level of protection from unwanted interference by the white establishment opposed to the school (Bonastia 146–47).

On the surface, the formation of a board with both Black and white participants appeared to highlight the importance of integration, but the individual commitments of trustees further demonstrated the complexities of the rhetorical situation. Trustees had varied histories and commitments with regard to civil rights. In particular, Darden's relationship with integration was perhaps most concerning. His admittance of Blacks to the University of Virginia's law school during his tenure as dean was juxtaposed by a legacy of consistently voicing his willingness to uphold segregation at the K–12 level. However, Darden was thought to be an asset for the board because of his status as a former governor. This role ensured that he was a noted member in Virginia's patriarchal hierarchy. While the board had little to do with developing curriculum and pedagogy, its concentrated efforts at fundraising were integral to the school's budget. The school was designed from the beginning to be in existence for one year only, and the necessity of a $1 million budget was still a matter of concern because of the quick turnaround time. Funding came from an array of sources, with some of the larger amounts coming from the Ford Foundation, the Alfred P. Sloan Foundation, and the Danforth Foundation. Donations were also received from smaller funding agencies, corporate donors, and private individuals. In addition to funding, textbooks, supplies, and equipment were also donated.

Governor Harrison advised trustees during their first meeting, on August 17, 1963, that "the purpose of the Prince Edward Free School Association is not to deal with problems of segregation and integration. The purpose is to provide a first-class education for children to whom this opportunity has been denied" ("Minutes of First Meeting" 1). The specificity of his charge demonstrated an awareness of the way the Free School would be understood by many in the white community. Harrison's attempt to deflect the very issue that gave rise to the school was consistent with the rhetorical strategies of segregationists described in the previous chapter. He did not want the school or the board to assume that this was an opportunity to make statements about race. Ironically, the Free School was only necessary because Prince Edward's concept of citizenship was locked into an ideology that identified segregation as necessary for a healthy society.

Despite the governor's wishes for the Free School to *not* be perceived as a response to the county's *Brown* resistance, some whites in Prince Edward already viewed the school as intrusive to their community. An editorial appearing in the *Farmville Herald* just four days after the Free School trustees' first meeting, which took place on Tuesday, August 20, 1963, expressed concern that "the so-called 'Prince Edward Free School'" was being influenced by the federal government: "It would appear to us that there is enough teacher talent in Virginia to operate these schools successfully. The ability of the several members of the board and their experience would seem to us sufficient that they could direct the operation without the aid and influence of the U.S. Justice Department, the Health Education and Welfare department consultants of out-of-state universities, or teachers from any other state" ("Prince Edward Free Schools"). The concerns about where faculty and staff would come from stemmed from long-held distrust of outsiders coming in and interfering with southern ways of life. The time during the closures was a period in which Prince Edward saw an influx of outsiders providing support for the Black community—support that was often read by some whites as meddling and interference, as this editorial suggested.

Minutes from the board's first meeting indicate that there was "substantial discussion of the person or persons who might be appointed as the chief executive officer" ("Minutes of First Meeting"). Despite the board's desire to appoint a Virginian to this post, Neil Sullivan, who lived on Long Island in New York, would take the position. Sullivan came with a reputation for being a progressive leader in his community before taking this position with the Free School. He would also be an educational adviser to Sen. Robert F. Kennedy during his 1968 presidential campaign. During his time as superintendent for the Union Free School, a public school in East Williston, New York, on Long Island, he hired Black faculty to teach an all-white student body and advocated for innovative pedagogical practices such as ungraded grouping of students, which meant students were grouped by ability rather than by age. Yet, in spite of Sullivan's expressed commitments to racial equality, his tenure at the Free School would leave a complicated legacy.

Sullivan's arrival in Prince Edward in late summer 1963 came after a season of protests. As described in chapter 2, some of Prince Edward's Black youth began to protest and participate in sit-ins, much to the frustration of the white community, who had often spoken of a harmonious relationship between Blacks and whites in the community. From the beginning, Sullivan was adamant that Black youth should not antagonize the white community. During interviews for potential Free School teachers Sullivan described the types of demonstrations he wished to see: "Finally, I would say that we all have feelings about civil rights, and demonstrations seem to be the order of the day here in Farmville. But our job in the Free School is *teaching*—and teaching must be our way of demonstrating our convictions" (Sullivan, *Bound* 78). He believed that participation in sit-ins and demonstrations would cease if Black youth were able to return to school. There was a troubling inconsistency in Sullivan's desire not to antagonize the white community and the school's expressed objective to prepare students to be participants in democracy. If boycotts were a necessary means of expressing their concerns as citizens, then Sullivan was censuring the ways in which they could participate. Sullivan's teachers were a bit more understanding of the need to allow students to express citizenship in a variety of ways.

While Sullivan may have been altruistic in his intentions, his own reflections on Prince Edward and his involvement speak to his own complicated perspective. Sullivan's memoir is reflective of both the importance of his task in Prince Edward and an awareness that he brought bias with him. Sullivan's description of his first impression of Farmville's Black area showed his lack of familiarity with rural conditions: "I visited two sections in Farmville where many of the poorer Negroes lived. I drove into these ghetto areas, parked my car, and walked around. I was familiar with slum conditions in New York and Boston, but this tour gave me new insights into rural deprivation" (*Bound* 20). His description seems to demonstrate a lack of awareness about rural life for some Black southerners. A few pages later, he rethinks his perception as he reflects on his own surprise at visiting the home of a Black college president who would come to be part of the Free School Board: "The few time-worn stereotypes of Negroes which I may still have had in the recesses of my mind were quickly and completely wiped out. These people had charm, intelligence and great dignity" (42). In part, his reflections point to the differences he was not accustomed to, as well as his own intolerance that he had to address.

His memoir further demonstrates that Sullivan was struggling to come to terms with what it meant to live in a community that was very different from his home on Long Island. He described a less than genteel social climate during his stay in Virginia. For example, although Sullivan desired student displays of citizenship that could not be perceived as combative or hostile, he was welcomed into Prince Edward with prank calls and a shotgun blast beneath his bedroom window (Sullivan, *Bound* 100, 131). This was not the Virginia that most whites wanted described. In spite of his own prejudices and habits of exaggeration, Sullivan was committed to this endeavor. He left a comfortable position on Long Island and walked into chaos in Virginia.

Although he may have desired the school to neither provoke nor antagonize the white community, the Free School's presence loomed as an unwelcome response to the school closures. Sullivan recounted numerous threats and acts of intimidation he and the school's teachers experienced. At his home, Sullivan and his wife saw drivers racing cars in his driveway and blaring their horns at two in the morning. Unwanted visitors left garbage and cemetery floral arrangements on their lawn. During a trip out of state, the Sullivans' car, left in Prince Edward, was vandalized. Free School teachers from outside of the community received a similar welcome. From coldly brusque service in local stores to mass car-ticketing for those with out-of-state license plates, some in the county made known their displeasure at the presence of these visitors.

Historians also note that Sullivan was criticized after the Free School closed for what some believed to be exaggerations of his time spent in Prince Edward. After leaving the county, he was understood to have sometimes exaggerated portrayals of the county, students, and faculty. For example, outside of the county he was known to describe the Black students as nonverbal and living in ghetto-like conditions (Sullivan, *Bound* 20). These statements directly contradicted some of his observations found in archival materials. For example, Sullivan indicated in a November 1963 progress report to trustees that teaching staff had on average "eight years of experience in the field of education" ("November Progress Report," 4). The sources, when put into conversation with each other, depict a leader who should be applauded for his work at the Free School but who made egregious comments during his tenure. This is not a special circumstance related to Sullivan. It speaks more to the imperfection and fluctuations in the character of humans and the institutions they create.

The Difficulty of Design within Constraint

Sullivan worked under a tight deadline so the school could open by September 16, 1963. The board of trustees had only met twice by the end of August, and he did not relocate to Prince Edward until August 23, 1963 (Sullivan, *Bound* 3). In this short window of time, he had to secure buildings, draft a curriculum, hire and train teachers, and register students. Unlike PECCA's training centers that utilized improvised spaces, the Free School utilized rented school buildings and buses, which meant access to desks, blackboards, and playground equipment. Setting up schools in formerly segregated facilities for both Black and white children made a statement. Jessica Enoch theorizes that physical spaces hold meaning that influences our behaviors. Rhetorics of space "explain what the space should be, what it should do, and what should go on inside it" (Enoch, "Woman's

Place" 276). While PECCA's tutoring sessions and crash courses had been offered in church basements and community centers, the use of vacant public schools articulated in concrete terms that the Free School would be a *real* educational opportunity. The use of previously segregated school buildings further articulated the Free School's commitment to provide students with an integrated school experience, as students occupied classrooms that were once for whites only. Sullivan and Free School business manager W. H. Baldwin, a longtime white resident of Prince Edward who took the position knowing he would be viewed with suspicion by neighbors, were able to negotiate the rental of four buildings from the county: the formerly all-Black R. R. Moton High School and two small elementary schools, Mary E. Branch 1 and 2, along with a small formerly white high school, Worsham High, for $2,800, along with the use of twenty buses. These spaces and buses helped express the Free School's aim to be recognized as bringing educational access to all the students of Prince Edward regardless of race. The buildings held what Roxanne Mountford describes as "heuristic power": "Spaces have heuristic power over their inhabitants and spectators by forcing them to change both their behavior . . . and, sometimes, their view of themselves" (50). Using traditional school buildings made a statement to students, teachers, and the larger community that the Free School was to be a space for learning and that these students had a right to an education.

The task of recruiting teachers was the next priority. Sullivan cast a wide net to obtain the best possible pool of applicants. Letters were sent to fellow school superintendents, universities with teacher-training programs, the US Employment Service, the armed services, Peace Corps, National Education Association, and commercial employment agencies specializing in the education field. The trustees expressed their desire to make Free School jobs available to local teachers who had lost work when the schools closed, but this prospective pool of applicants was small; most of the white teachers were already employed by the segregation academy. Many Black teachers had left the community during the previous four years to seek employment elsewhere. Regardless of the circumstances, finding qualified teachers in August would have been a challenge because most teachers had contracts for the school year by this time. A week before classes, Sullivan's faculty roster totaled only 13, with the expectation that the school would welcome some 800 students; the actual enrollment would be almost double that figure, reaching 1,571. By the first day, September 16, the number of teachers rose to 35. Responding to a now desperate need, Virginia State University, an HBCU about sixty miles east of Prince Edward, sent students from its school of education to cover temporary classroom gaps. By November, the roster of teachers would include Blacks and whites from across the country, making it Virginia's first fully integrated teaching body.

Teacher applications from the Free School archive show that there were many applicants who articulated a sense of wanting to help the community as the main impetus for applying to teach at the Free School. One applicant, Duane Jones, described his desire to teach in the Free School as a "moral commitment." In Jones's letter of application, he wrote, "Aside from these factors of qualification, I feel a personal as well as moral commitment to Prince Edward County which probably needs to be explained no further than to say that as a Negro educator I feel that this is what I must do and this is where I must be for as long as I can be of ultimate value" (6). There were others who attempted to obtain positions out of curiosity or even out of desperation for work. Others, like Katherine Whittaker, cited their faith as a motive for applying: "I am a Quaker and as such I am interested in helping with the education of children who have not been able to obtain schooling for the last four years." There were some whose applications raised legitimate concerns because of criminal records, problems with alcohol, or prior dismissal from other school systems (Sullivan, *Bound* 56). Ultimately, the Free School faculty roster would be complete with ninety-seven teachers across four school buildings. The integrated staff would comprise eighty-two teachers identifying as African Americans and fifteen identifying as Caucasian ("Teacher Roster").

Much of Sullivan's success in supporting and mentoring teachers derived from two of his earliest hires: James B. Cooley, upper unit principal, and Willie Mae Watson, the director of elementary education. Watson and Cooley were instrumental in localizing Sullivan's curriculum to make it relevant for the students in Prince Edward and in leading professional development efforts for teachers. Cooley came from nearby Brunswick County, where he had worked as an assistant principal for the county's all-Black high school. He took a year's leave of absence from his position to serve as lead principal for the upper unit of the Free School. Watson, a former Peace Corps volunteer and school administrator from Norfolk, Virginia, brought a wealth of experience and energy to the program. Sullivan remarked that Watson "radiated spirit and zest, and she had the courage to match her convictions" (*Bound* 62). As Black educators from Virginia, Watson and Cooley had a level of familiarity with Prince Edward that Sullivan lacked. While the board set the goals for the Free School to be a temporary measure and Sullivan organized the institutional structure and logistics, it was Cooley and Watson who adapted the curricula to make the experience match the day-to-day needs of this most unique group of students and teachers.

In addition to recruiting teachers, Sullivan's time was also spent canvassing for students. Registration would begin before the school was even fully staffed. In his formal efforts to encourage enrollments, Sullivan would visit the local radio station, WFLO, to announce the school's opening. He had less control over coverage in the local press. The *Farmville Herald* carried editorials that ranged from a lukewarm acknowledgment of students having access to education again to objections aired about the Department of Justice's "do gooders" interfering with the people of Prince Edward ("Around Robin Hood's Barn). Dr. Moss, aforementioned supporter and ally, worried that the Free School wasn't being presented in local news coverage as being a "total" school system that was integrated, and he wrote to board member Darden out of concern that the *Herald* was "attempting to keep this information from the county's citizens" (C. Moss, Letter). Darden reassured Moss that newspaper coverage outside of Farmville acknowledged the Free School's unique offering to the community. There is no way to know if Moss was satisfied by this response, but it is interesting that Darden acknowledged the news coverage from outside of the community.

Many in the Black community heard about the Free School from time spent in church and from adults who were privy to conversations about the goings-on of the community. Enrollment from the Black community began early and was strong. Sullivan cited the "long lines of children with their parents" who came to register and receive a free back-to-school physical exam (Sullivan, *Bound* 60). It feels important to mention here that the Free School did in fact reach its goal of being integrated not only with regard to faculty but its student body as well. There would be a total of eight white students who attended across the upper and lower units. Sullivan certainly acknowledged that this would be an integrated space, but there was always question and concern about how many white children would attend. If the school was designed to be a response to those who were without an education, undoubtedly that audience was primarily Black, given the high numbers of white families who sent their children to the segregation academy.

White student enrollments trickled in, with a total of four for the first day. They included Professor Moss's son, Dickie, and Letitia Tew, whose parents were adamant that schooling should be free (Sullivan, *Bound* 82). Additionally, George and Brenda Abernathy, whose family was new to Prince Edward County, having come from Portsmouth, Virginia, would enroll just before school began. The Abernathy family approached Sullivan very discreetly. Sullivan would describe being passed a message indicating he should reach out to Mr. Abernathy, who insisted on a private meeting with no publicity. Sullivan would meet with Abernathy on the same day as the Sixteenth Street Baptist Church bombing in Alabama. Abernathy told Sullivan that he wanted a good education for his kids and that he favored free education, "integrated or not" (98). Having had his family experience integrated schools in Portsmouth, Abernathy wasn't opposed to them, but he did fear for his children's safety attending the Free School, given Prince Edward's racial climate. The school's white enrollment would double after the Christmas holiday, when the Lewis family sent their four children: Thomas, Betty Jo, Edith Ann, and James. Longtime residents of Prince Edward, the Lewis family could not afford the segregated academy's tuition and were not opposed to integrated schools; however, they worried about the response of neighbors. Finally, persuaded by the desire to have his children back in school, Mr. Lewis told Sullivan, "I haven't wanted to be rebellious to the community, but now I want my kids back in school. I just can't hold them out any longer to keep anybody's feelings from being hurt" (qtd. in Sullivan, *Bound* 181–82). This example best describes the kind of tenuous situation Sullivan had to navigate with regard to recruitment. There was little that he could promise with regard to calming white fears about rattling the community. For the few white parents who did send their students to the Free School, there was great risk involved in taking this action.[2] In addition to securing enrollment and reassuring parents, however, Sullivan needed a curriculum to serve this most unique group of students and their community.

Policies and Procedures for a Herculean Task

Stuart Blythe, scholar of rhetoric and technical communication, encourages us to understand how institutions work, and what individual and collaborative agency within these groups looks like, by turning our attention to texts that seem

Figure 5. Students and adults gathered outside Free School No. 2 (Mary E. Branch School) for registration, Farmville, Virginia [undated]. Farmville 1963 Civil Rights Protests, Virginia Commonwealth University James Branch Cabell Library. Special Collections and Archives.

"mundane." Blythe writes of the effects documents have on the labor involved in agency and how they obtain power through the ways in which they are "written, presented, and received" in an institution (181–82). Further, Blythe reminds us that institutions are maintained through documents and that to better understand how institutions operate and influence, we should study their documents. My analysis of the Free School's handbook demonstrates that the institution's primary aims were to mobilize teachers to take on this unique situation, provide guidelines for basic classroom interaction, and to express unyielding commitment to serve this group of students. Throughout the description of policies and procedures three themes become apparent in the Free School's handbook: the importance of displaying respect to students, the role of literacy in facilitating democratic participation, and the responsibility of teachers to consistently reflect and modify their pedagogical practices. These themes were essential for the Free School and were indicative of a philosophy of learning that gave students an experience outside the turbulent context of Massive Resistance. While these ideas were not unique to educators, they took on a different meaning given the conditions in Prince Edward. Moreover, as the next section will show, the curriculum, pedagogy, and philosophy that created the foundation of the Free School were a unique reflection of both the new research coming from the education field and the time-honored traditions found in segregated Black schools. Before I present these documents and how they guided teachers' effort and affected incoming students, I provide context on the trends and general landscape of public education during the middle of the twentieth century. This background will situate the Free School experience both within and outside of the educational trends that were developing nationally.

The years leading up to the 1960s saw major change in America's public schools in addition to integration. Growing numbers of students meant a demand for state and federal funds. The disproportion between rural and urban areas and Black and white schools often resulted in a wide disparity between the kinds of resources that were made available. The end of World War I was a time when people began to understand the need for creating national standards in public education, because it was seen as a means by which to produce patriotic citizens who could be trained to work. The National Education Association (NEA) was formed to promote research and change in education. The Cardinal Principles of Secondary Education, objectives crafted by the NEA, were one such method to standardize high schools across the nation. Additionally, progressive views about education continued to develop alongside this effort at standardization and promoting nationalism. While progressive ideas about education were trumpeted by John Dewey, William H. Kilpatrick, George Counts, and others during the late 1890s and into the early twentieth century, the ideas never took hold in American public schools because most educational institutions attempted to achieve cultural uniformity rather than diversity. Progressive educators valued student-centered learning experiences that accounted for the individual nature of each student in developing a critically engaged citizenry. The primary proponent of progressive education, Dewey, believed that rather than have students learn through instruction, they should learn through experiences that would meet the needs of a constantly changing society. For Dewey, education was a growth process that recognized the unique individuality of each child through student-centered classrooms. In spite of the desire of some educators to create these student-centered classrooms, traditional notions about education, which often privileged teacher-centered learning (rote memorization, direct instruction, test-driven results, etc.) remained common. During World War II and the Cold War, cultural conservatism silenced progressive education because people feared that America would be left vulnerable and behind in the face of an increasingly technologically oriented society.

The years following World War II made a large impact on public education. Having been confronted with fighting against Germany and Japan, the United States was also confronted with its own horrors of racism. Establishing itself as a superpower, the United States became the torchbearer for spreading democracy around the world, but there was much work to be done at home. These years were the backdrop for the NAACP's introduction of a strategy for integration cases and for the American public's emerging recognition that racism was a problem not only on foreign soil. Following World War II, the Cold War era brought heightened awareness of nuclear war and fear of the spread of communism. Critiques about public education spread rapidly. Rudolf Flesch's *Why Johnny Can't Read* (1955) urged a back-to-basics movement to remedy what he saw as poor literacy education in public schools. With the launching of Sputnik by the Soviets in 1957, the public education system was blamed for making the United States lag behind in scientific and technological advancement. William J. Reese, a historian of education, describes the spirit of fear and desperation embedded in coverage about the educational crisis in the United States during the early 1950s: not enough elementary schools, not enough teachers, standards not on par with the rest of the world (Reese 219). There were growing concerns over Soviet technological and scientific advancements and that Americans would fall behind. The general consensus that was public education needed to bolster teaching quality and course offerings for students to be able to compete in this new world. Teaching students the "three Rs" (reading, writing, and reckoning, or arithmetic) with stronger math programs became the primary focus. This approach was seen as being best for students who needed an intellectually challenging environment if the United States was to come out on top during the Cold War. Many critics of American education focused on keeping up with the pace of other nations. The Black community in particular was invested in having schools fulfill their promise of graduating students who were fully active and engaged citizens in the country. As Reese notes, these battles were waged in the public sphere through civil rights leaders, "but the struggle occurred at the grassroots level, community by community, where most of the activists led modest lives and thus had much to lose" (227). The Free School was a product of this era, and the curricula reflected a unique need to attend to pressing national as well as local concerns. As my analysis of the documents from the Free School will show, this particular institution was a unique amalgamation of then-new public education trends in the areas of grouping and assessment, a legacy of Black teachers who believed in providing students with challenging educations despite having few resources and of the civil rights movement's demand for recognition of Blacks as full citizens of the United States.

The Free School handbook addressed the infrastructure of both the upper and lower units. The lower unit comprised three school buildings (Branch 1, Branch 2, and Worsham) and served the needs of students ages six through twelve. The upper unit, housed in the Robert Russa Moton High School building, accommodated students ages thirteen to twenty-one, with further division between students ages thirteen to sixteen and seventeen to twenty-one. The handbook opens with a letter of welcome in which Sullivan describes the "Herculean" task teachers at the Free School would face: "Are we individually and collectively strong enough to meet the demands of this multi-dimensional educational problem? Only time will tell and only our combined best effort will give us the chance to succeed." In this statement, he expresses the importance of teachers in achieving the school's goals. He urges teachers, administrators, and staff to forget the norms of conventional schools "and realistically come to grips with our unique problem." His call to forget the norms was a reflection of the need to adopt a variety of practices for working with the Free School students. Sullivan proposed that the school could "help us close this intolerable gap," referencing segregated schools that had always been unequal, through its use of "proven innovations and methods" such as ungraded classrooms and team teaching.

In light of the way Prince Edward County's whites treated Black students in 1963, Sullivan's exhortation to teachers "to assume full responsibility immediately; to exercise good common sense in dealing with every situation; to treat these youngsters with kindness, tact and dignity; to prepare everything with the greatest care; to dedicate yourself completely to meeting the needs of the individual child" was reflective of progressive student-centered commitments to learning. As previously described, while ideas about progressive education had been in retreat after the Cold War, Sullivan realized a need to develop curricula that were not just focused on producing a citizenry that could make the United States more technologically advanced but that could welcome students. Sullivan's stance, at least as reflected in this statement, demonstrated a commitment to the latter. Given the treatment these students had previously suffered at the hands of local government, his statement described a stance for teachers to embody that was an affront to Massive Resistance because, for once, Black children were being put in the center (Sullivan, "Prince Edward County Free School Association" [Handbook]).

Central to Sullivan's handbook were eight educational objectives used to shape the school's curriculum. Titled "Objectives of Education" and "Imperative Needs of Youth," Sullivan's objectives did not cite sources but were derived from the National Association of Secondary-School Principals' Committee on Curriculum Planning and Development. These objectives were published by the group as the "Ten Common and Essential Needs That All Youth Have in a Democratic Society," also known as the "Ten Imperative Needs of Youth." The original document, drafted in 1944, focused on what educators believed to be important for the production of global citizens. The committee sought to present educators with "plans for postwar education" (*Cardinal Principles* xv). The needs ranged from physical education and fitness, understanding the significance of family, how to purchase goods and services, and the importance of science, to an explicit call for youth to understand what it means to be a citizen. The central theme was loyalty to democracy and the belief that critical literacy could inform and protect democratic processes. Three objectives from Sullivan's objectives most clearly demonstrate the aims and suggested direction for teaching citizenship in the Free School. The first objective clearly outlined the school's dedication to American democracy:

1. To promote loyalty to principles upon which our democracy was founded.

a. Content should develop an interest in and understanding of basic American culture along with technological advancements, which have affected our way of life. Students should learn that there are obligations connected with our various freedoms if our democracy is to be preserved and perpetuated.

It seems obvious that a school sponsored in part by the federal government would promote democracy and loyalty to the United States. But this mission is difficult when the commitment to democracy must be taught in an environment where "good" citizenship was often equated with white supremacist ideology. If students were to learn about the "obligations connected with our various freedoms," then the Free School's very existence was itself a lesson.

Promoting loyalty to democracy, of course, was not a phenomenon particular to the Free School. As previously discussed, the very purpose of public schooling in the United States has long been to normalize students into democratic citizens. As the conversations I describe in chapter 1 suggest, the behaviors and loyalty ascribed to good citizenship have most often been predetermined by those in power, to protect their interests. Further, this spoke to the kind of post–World War II ethos that emphasized the importance of national unity, assimilation, and patriotism. What this process looked like and how citizens were to be prepared has varied according to what types of citizenship practice are valued by a particular community. To nurture a connection between students and American democracy in the Free School required an acknowledgment on the part of teachers and administration that students had to first experience and witness being respected by an institution claiming to be founded upon these concepts, because many of the institutional structures connected with democracy had traditionally prohibited real participation by members of Prince Edward's Black community. The Free School was also a place where Black students in particular could witness and experience respect and acknowledgment of their personhood in a way that was similar to what they had experienced in Black spaces. This, however, was different because it was a place that was integrated. This is not to suggest that Black Prince Edwardians did not have their own spaces for practicing and engaging in citizenship. As will be discussed in the next chapter, Black churches and homes were spaces where members were able to hold agency away from the watchful eyes of whites. Free School teachers and administrators needed to consciously display respect to both the students and the communities from which they came to make this goal meaningful. As examples in this chapter will show, it was a goal that was not always met. How students were perceived by faculty and what type of curriculum was believed to be best for this student population were two of the primary areas where dissension among administrators and teachers occurred.

Sullivan's second objective really furthered the notion that students would promote loyalty to American democracy and culture in their communities. The objective reads as follows:

2. To develop respect for and appreciation of the community in which we live.

a. Content should establish and reinforce an understanding of our historical background and growth. Local resources and resource programs within the community should be fully utilized.

Meeting this goal would no doubt be a challenge. What did it mean to ask students to be respectful and appreciate the community in which they lived? The community was divided, and those in power showed little respect. One way to try to improve the relationships between students and their community was through field trips. Sullivan viewed the local community as a resource for students to experience. Teachers took students on field trips to the local bank, the post office, and the fire station. Student explorations were not limited to Prince Edward County. His memoir describes opportunities that allowed the Free School students to "see beyond the imprisoning environment they had always known in Prince Edward County" (Sullivan, *Bound* 184). Granting students time to experience these public spaces that either law or custom deemed "whites only" was instrumental to the school's mission of using community resources and testifying that the students belonged in these spaces.[3] Students visited "cultural, historic, business, and industrial centers" ("Field Trips" 7). Longer excursions included trips to Washington, DC, Monticello, and Jamestown, sites that stand as symbols of freedom and democracy.

Additionally, teachers played an important role in unpacking this objective and finding ways to have students see themselves as part of the larger history of Prince Edward. Teachers did this by giving students opportunities that taught them about the local Black community's legacy of civic engagement. Notably, the structure for doing this unpacking came from Cooley and Watson, Black educators who embodied tactics that often made Black teachers successful in less than stellar conditions. In *Black Teachers on Teaching*, Michele Foster suggests that the commitment of Black teachers to Black students helped to create significant connections between students and their communities. In spite of the "difficult circumstances," Foster argues, Black teachers committed to Black students were able to "struggle against (and help their students struggle against) all forms of racial oppression, and to build a sense of connection between students and their communities" (xii). Watson did just this by creating a pamphlet that described important public figures in Prince Edward's Black community. Her resource highlighted significant moments in Prince Edward's history ranging from Black representation at the Constitutional Convention to postemancipation efforts to establish better educational opportunities. This history lesson placed the experience of the Black community at the center rather than the margins. Students were taught to understand the Black community as active agents rather than passive recipients of white benevolence or oppression.

Sullivan's third objective emphasized the school's commitment to using literacy as a method of both preserving and encouraging democratic participation. His aim to use literacy as a vehicle for citizenship was reflective of an understanding of literacy as a precursor to democratic engagement:

3. To promote the improvement and preservation of our democratic form of government through a literate populace.

a. Literacy presumes more than the teaching of the "3 R's." It presumes training to think and observe carefully, and the effort to formulate answers that are important to our civilization. Content must influence students to think clearly, so as to be able to sift the truths from the untruths when scrutinizing our democratic processes as well as the governmental processes of other world peoples.

This objective reveals the scope of literacy as the Free School envisioned it. Rather than rote skills and memorization, the curriculum stressed the development of analytical thought as a necessity for democratic practice. This emphasis demonstrated a desire to recognize students as more than empty vessels to be filled and to highlight their inherent dignity as learners. Using a more progressive learning perspective would help to reassure students who had been without any consistent access to educational spaces that literacy could be a means by which expressions of citizenship are made. It did not, however, necessarily account for the demonstrations of citizenship that many of these students had witnessed in their parents' fight for their own education in the county. As will be explored in the following chapter, some Free School students gained their first knowledge about the practices of citizenship at home and in their churches. The belief that clear thought was necessary to delineate truth suggested a faith in rational liberal democracy, if the proper skills were in place. Teachers utilized a scaffolded language arts curriculum that sought to meet students at multiple levels within each class. This curriculum utilized a pedagogy that recognized both the unique situation of these students and the importance of literacy for the Black community.

Literacy instruction included lessons in phonics and grammar, drills, themed writing exercises, and oral recitation (Cooley, "Prince Edward Moton Handbook" 2; Sullivan *Bound* 63). In this way, the Free School instituted instructional practices similar to those used in public schools across the country. Literacy curricula from the 1960s and their description of approaches to reading, writing, and speaking in public schools indicate it was an era when basal readers, sight words, and instruction in phonics were on the rise (Allington and McGill-Franzen 3; Pearson 419). New methods in phonics instruction, or teaching the sounds associated with letters, provides students with the ability to decode and read words. This compilation of techniques—controlled vocabulary readers, a shift away from oral recitation toward silent reading, and phonics—were some of the most popular methods employed in public schools.

The Free School's focus on providing a literacy program comparable to that of white counterparts across the country belied the arguments of some whites implying that Black community members lacked a true desire to receive an education. It also testified to the Black community's desire to obtain the skills that democracy requires. Watson and Cooley helped to translate Sullivan's objectives into real everyday practices.

Fighting for access to literacy has been part of the Black experience since slavery, when forced illiteracy prevented them from writing passes that might allow their free movement and escape. Beyond this, Heather Andrea Williams describes the intrinsic power and possibility of literacy for Blacks during the antebellum period in *Self-Taught: African American Education in Slavery and Freedom*. Reading and writing offered opportunities to "disturb the power relations between master and slave, as they fused their desire for literacy with their desire for freedom" (Williams 7). These attempts to obtain literacy would not readily secure the immediate recognition of equality in the eyes of whites, but as Shirley Wilson Logan demonstrates, the acquisition of literacy and "rhetorical astuteness" allows Blacks "to negotiate a hostile environment" (3). This history of self-determination in Black schooling is far from a simple story. While there has been general consensus in the Black community about the importance of education, there has been consistent debate about how that education should look, and the Free School was no exception. The long-standing debate about the purpose education should serve for the Black community is frequently associated with the poles of Booker T. Washington and W. E. B. Du Bois. Both Du Bois and Washington were shaped by their own environments and relationships with education. Du Bois was raised a free man in the North and Washington was born a slave on a plantation in the South. An oversimplification of their arguments relates that Du Bois valued education as a means by which a select group of Blacks (known as the talented tenth) could prosper through careers as doctors, lawyers, and teachers. At the other end of the debate, Washington preferred vocational training and encouraged the Black community to concentrate on uplift primarily through industrial trades, farming, and craftwork. These two positions dominated conversations in the late nineteenth and early twentieth centuries about education and the Black community. While I do not attempt to draw a conclusion that the Kennedy administration, which was tasked with helping to organize the Free School, or the Free School board, or Sullivan were having conversations that involved Du Bois or Washington, some of the choices Cooley and Watson advocated for harken back to these larger debates. Certainly gaining access to literacy never resulted in automatic recognition of citizenship. It has, however, represented self-determination, self-improvement, and power. The Free School's decision to use a traditional language arts program, one that would have mirrored the curriculum of white schools, announced the school's commitment to providing students with as close to a traditional education as the circumstances made possible. Further, it demonstrated what Black students were capable of doing.

Following his treatment on the schools' objectives, Sullivan prefaces a list of "ten points" to outline "the development of our curriculum and the relationship between lay and professional groups working under my direction in Prince Edward County." The overarching theme of this list is a belief that the curriculum was "integral" to the "total school program" and involved a consistent assessment and input from multiple stakeholders. Sullivan's points reveal a design that was open to contributions from various stakeholders: "Plan of organization must make it possible for anyone to make a suggestion—and have [that] suggestion come directly to those responsible." His lists of stakeholders also included "parents-citizens-lay groups," groups who could make a "valuable contribution" ("Prince Edward County Free School Association" [Handbook] 4). This move speaks to an understanding on his part to not let the school be a space implemented by outsiders and thus without any input from others invested in the community. How this was implemented with regard to parents is difficult to ascertain. The Free School archive contained newsletters and announcements that were sent home to communicate important dates, school functions, and other general information. It was not clear how parent feedback was requested outside of PTA meetings, for which no minutes were found, and, if feedback was provided, how the school responded. As will be discussed, materials from the archive show that Sullivan incorporated feedback from the American Friends Service Committee, whose members made recommendations about the best course of action for providing programming opportunities for the older youth who might be interested in vocational training.

Sullivan's list describes a structure for organizing curriculum planning and input: "Work is best carried forward by small groups representing the total group, which concentrates upon specific problems." Free School teachers found themselves divided into curriculum planning groups for primary subjects (language arts, mathematics, and science) that reported back to curriculum leaders. As I will demonstrate in the sections on the curricula for the upper and lower units, the curriculum leaders held meetings and issued bulletins on these meetings' work. These documents were used to both record and report the work of these groups, as well as to announce changes that were to be implemented. Sullivan also emphasized that curriculum improvement should employ a team approach, which would complement the team-teaching approach ("Prince Edward County Free School Association" [Handbook] 4).

Following the philosophy and curriculum points, Sullivan's handbook was full of helpful hints for teachers, especially for getting a good start to the first day. Guidelines for the first day, titled "A Good Start," advocated for teachers spending time getting to know the community and the school buildings, as well as becoming familiar with the supplies in the classroom. Perhaps most important were the suggestions he provided for getting to know the children: "Learn their names as fast as you can. Then work hard to learn as much about them as possible. Use all available means—records, report cards, health cards, etc." For any class, building community is integral, but for these students something as simple as learning their names would have been an important first step for developing good teacher-student relationships. Continuing with the theme of building healthy teacher-student relations, Sullivan advised, "Win their confidence. Have them tell about themselves. Tell them what supplies they will need. Give them an overview of the year's work. Teach something now [sic] the first day" ("Prince Edward County Free School Association" [Handbook] 5). For students who'd been without access to formal education for four years, there was undoubtedly a need to give them space for sharing who they were as well as what to expect. Again, laying the groundwork for pedagogical practices that would celebrate the students was not new, but in this context it took on new meaning because it boldly claimed that these students were valued in this space.

Following guidelines for the first day, a section called "Improvement of Assignment" provided direction for the types of assignments that were developed. Reflecting on then-current educational practices, Sullivan writes, "Today, the aims of mental discipline through memorization of subject matter, of knowledge for its own sake, are giving way to the aims of furthering the growth in the pupil of desirable understandings, attitudes and appreciations, and abilities useful in organized society. The assignment is aimed not so much at mastery of subject matter as at the use of subject matter in experiences which enhance growth" ("Prince Edward County Free School Association" [Handbook] 6). Sullivan's explanation suggests a belief in learning through experience rather than rote memorization for testing purposes and highlights long-standing foundations that ground progressive and critical pedagogies. Foregrounding the desire to have students do work that would help them develop not only academic but personal qualities as well speaks to an awareness of students as individuals who are part of multiple communities. This section contained a list of twelve principles for generating and assessing assignments. Sullivan acknowledged that the principles were "based on several lists found in scattered sources" ("Prince Edward County Free School Association" [Handbook] 6).

Taken together, the twelve principles convey a desire to have teachers craft assignments that were clear in their objectives. He reminds teachers that "the objective, the thing to be done, should be stated in clear, simple language." Building upon the principle that students needed to feel connected to their studies, he advises that "a provocative and convincing connection should be made between the subject matter of the assignment and the typical activities, interests, and the needs of the pupils' current lives." This principle also rested on the need for teachers who were not familiar with the students of Prince Edward County to spend time getting to know them and learning about their community. Crucial to this principle was also the need to account for the varying academic levels of students coming into the Free School. Sullivan noted this when he advocated for assignments that would "provide for different levels of achievements, for greater varied study of learning activities, in accord with the range of differences in ability, interests, and needs within the group" ("Prince Edward County Free School Association" [Handbook] 8). His use of team teaching was another a response. Partnering teachers allowed for students to be further divided into groups in the classroom according to ability. Continuing along the lines of developing student-centered assignments, Sullivan provides a principle that highlights allowing students input in the generating of assignments: "Pupil participation in selecting and developing assignments and methods of procedures is definitely desirable" ("Prince Edward County Free School Association" [Handbook] 8). What distinguished the nongraded structure as being different from traditional graded K–12 structure were beliefs about teaching and student development. Proponents of the nongraded classroom believed that these environments were more accurate reflections of the ways in which students grew and developed. In the traditional graded model, students' progress is seen as being unified and advancing in regular fashion across all areas of development. In the nongraded structure, there was more flexibility, as a student could excel in one area and need more assistance in another subject. The nongraded structure provided teachers with a longitudinal view of curriculum with more attention placed on continuity and sequence (Goodlad and Anderson 80). In a space such as this, teachers were not bound to follow predetermined packaged curricula, and there was no expectation that all students would consume the curriculum at the same time and in the same way. This kind of environment sought to capitalize on the natural growth and development of the children to facilitate their learning in the classroom.

Sullivan's description follows the fundamentals presented by John Goodlad and Robert Anderson. He began with instructions for teachers to use during the first weeks of school: "study pupil records; evaluate student performance; formulate plans for grouping" (Sullivan, "Bulletin #9" 2). Citing scholarship that defines team teaching, he explicitly draws from Robert Anderson's May 1961 article in the *Journal of the National Education Association* on team teaching. Sullivan defined team teaching as "a group of several teachers jointly responsible for planning, carrying out, and evaluating an educational program for a group of children" ("Bulletin #9" 4). Sullivan's list of the advantages of team teaching included both practical and pedagogical rationales directly related to the Free School's context. Team teaching allowed for more experienced teachers to reach larger groups of students and to have assistance in carrying out group work, thus allowing for new teachers to "study under the more experienced teachers." From the perspective of students, team teaching provided them with multiple options for grouping in the classroom: "[i]nstructional grouping of almost any size and composition can be arranged" (3). Sullivan also advanced the importance of non-graded schools for students to "grow at their own growth pattern" (4). The flexibility that allowed students to move through the curriculum at their own pace and provided access to both small and large group instruction was important because it offered particular benefits to students who had been without consistent access to formal education.

The Free School students were thus grouped by age and then ability with the option of moving in between grades. For example, nine- and ten-year-olds might be grouped together in the elementary school and then subdivided by ability. Once students mastered a particular skill, they were able to advance to the next group or level. In theory, this would allow for students to move as quickly through the curriculum as they were able or to spend as much time in certain subject areas as their skill set demanded. Because students of the same age might enter the Free School at different levels of mastery in spite of age and having had different life experiences during the school closures, there was a need to implement a program that would allow for flexibility. While nongraded classrooms were not the norm in most public schools, they were a response that helped to mitigate the complexities of the Free School students' particular situations.

Encouraging his teachers to develop a stance in the classroom whereby students were co-collaborators in knowledge and assessment practices that dealt gently with students was a bold proclamation that indicated hope for classroom experiences that were not dominated by teacher knowledge. Likewise, the "Testing and Evaluation" section describes traditional testing procedures (essays, standardized tests, problem-situation tests) but is prefaced with a reminder that "the modern teacher uses many of these new techniques, and with the participation of pupils develops still others fitted to the specific needs of the situation" (Sullivan, "Prince Edward County Free School Association" [Handbook] 8). Rather than blindly implement testing procedures that may or may not fit the needs of the students, teachers could follow the handbook guideline suggesting that they be reflective about their testing processes. This was imperative for developing classrooms that would meet the needs of students with varying academic levels and experiences. Sullivan also reminded teachers who used practice drills to make such work "meaningful" and to use them only in situations where memorization was actually warranted. Understanding that skills and drills practices were often tedious for students, he admonishes teachers to make practice periods "live, interesting, and pleasant" ("Prince Edward County Free School Association" [Handbook] 9).

The handbook's final section described trends and beliefs about discipline. Arranged to showcase pairings of older disciplinary techniques among new best practices, the list included eleven trends in classroom discipline techniques. These included such things as moving away from the use of loud commands to the use of softer voices, and from less planning *for* students to making plans *with* students. Once more, Sullivan privileged a type of collaboration between teachers and students that positioned students as active agents in their learning. Sullivan's handbook provided a framework and the general direction and mission of the program. His vision for a school that welcomed students of varying abilities, centered student experiences in the classroom, and pushed teachers to negotiate a stance that placed them as co-creators of knowledge with their students certainly could not be carried out alone. The team-teaching and nongraded structure provided the context for this plan to unfold.

Sullivan's handbook, the team-teaching approach, and the school's nongraded structure provided the global mission for the school, but it was the work of Watson and Cooley that provided teachers with a localized understanding of how to accomplish the missions and goals via curricular practices best suited for their students. Watson, Cooley, and the teachers under their tutelage established classrooms where cultural awareness infused a traditional K–12 curriculum. This approach demonstrated an understanding of the need to counter the remaining effects of Massive Resistance through curricular design and pedagogical practice in three ways: (1) teachers reinforced the importance of the student's self-worth, (2) classroom and extracurricular activities honored the epistemological practices students brought from their home communities, and (3) a traditional approach to teaching core subjects challenged the notion that Black students were unable to perform at the level of their white counterparts. Watson and Cooley's approaches were not unlike those of other Black educators who were committed to Black children and their communities. Contemporary recovery efforts provide more nuanced understandings of how the complex past of segregated schooling has worked to dismiss the notion that segregated schools automatically meant inferior teachers. As Vanessa Siddle Walker reminds us, "The environment of the segregated school had affective traits, institutional policies, and community support that helped Black children learn in spite of the neglect their schools received" (3). Watson and Cooley were able to bring enthusiasm and a commitment to working with the Black community into their positions. Their careful adaptation of Sullivan's policies and procedures moved his mission from mere words to concrete action.

Willie Mae Watson's Guidelines for Curriculum Development

As director of elementary education for the Free School, Willie Mae Watson had two elementary school buildings with a total of thirty-seven teachers and some eight hundred students under her charge. She strove to provide students with every chance to have as close to a mainstream school experience as possible. She championed tutoring services for students who came into the school at all levels of learning. As the reflections from former students in chapter 5 will show, for those who had had opportunities to continue their learning since 1959 the Free School experience was another stepping stone in their educational journey. However, for those who had been entirely away from academic education—perhaps working in the fields or helping to take care of younger siblings—coming back into the classroom may have felt like a jump across a vast river. Watson anticipated these problems and met them head on through the curricula she developed and the mentoring of teachers under her direction. The documents she wrote (the lower unit's curriculum guide, teaching bulletins, Black history pamphlets, and professional development resource documents) emphasize the value of welcoming the knowledge and experiences of elementary students, providing culturally relevant teaching materials, and treating students with respect. Both are hallmarks of Dewey's theories on progressive education and central tenets adopted by many Black teachers who taught in segregated schools and for whom demonstrating to their students that they could achieve in spite of the hard realities of racism was part of their daily teaching (Foster 35). These themes were the quintessential aspects of the Free School's supportive educational environment. In context, they spoke back to the white supremacist ideologies that had created the educational crisis in Prince Edward.

Watson developed a detailed curriculum guide for the Free School's lower unit that translated Sullivan's objectives, as expressed in the schoolwide handbook, into specific classroom practices. Her "Guidelines to Curriculum Development for Primary School and Middle School" directly challenged stereotypes about Black students and the learning experiences that would benefit them. In this document, Watson describes the importance of offering curricular "unity" throughout the lower unit. She suggests that the guidelines "might be a common approach toward improving the learning experiences of children" (ii). The eight-page bulletin outlines each subject of study in the lower school: language arts, which included listening, speaking, reading, and writing; arithmetic; social studies; science; music; physical education; and a speech program for students with communication disorders. Watson also lists a description for content, aims, and outcomes for each subject. The aims and content descriptions reveal that Watson intended to implement a rigorous curriculum that would do more than compensate for lost time, despite early exchanges between Sullivan and the board that suggested that the Free School would provide only tutoring and remedial instruction, which was not an uncommon theme in the history of African American education. The lower unit's comprehensive curriculum was neither remedial nor removed from understanding the lived experiences of this unique group of students. In this way, the traditional curriculum spoke back to claims some in the white community circulated that Black students were not capable of mastering skills beyond manual labor.

Watson's respect for student needs is evident in the curriculum memos she frequently distributed to teachers. Through these memos the curriculum evolved during the school year, with Watson refining her understanding of the needs of both teachers and students. When put in conversation with teacher reflections from the archive, Watson's curriculum guide and memos exemplify the successes and struggles of both teachers and students in the Free School.

The language arts curriculum expressed Watson's respect for students more strongly than any other. She emphasized helping students to recognize their self-worth through reading and writing about subjects that were of interest to them. Following Sullivan's call for a school that would aid students in developing literacy skills that encouraged analysis, reflection, and response, the language arts curriculum guide encompassed classwork in listening, speaking, reading, and writing. Each set of aims and outcomes listed in the curriculum values both the mastery of skill and attention to cultivating self-respect. In relation to teaching children to listen, for example, Watson catalogs the following aims:

I. To help the child enjoy and increase his knowledge of the world about him.

II. To help the child learn new words.

III. To help the child learn new uses for the words he knows.

IV. To help develop good listening skills. ("Guidelines to Curriculum" 1)

Listening was a means for children to expand their knowledge about the world. Watson's language also emphasizes pleasure in knowledge, a sign of respect for students' own inclinations that would be likely to lead them to a productive path in education. Watson's recommendation for ways to practice listening indicates that students were to use these experiences as a means to become active participants in learning and sharing knowledge about their world. She calls on teachers to give students multiple opportunities to practice:

I. Listening in [an] audience situation.

II. Listening to communication media.

III. Listening to oneself for self-improvement. ("Guidelines to Curriculum" 1)

Recognizing the importance of a variety of listening situations—not just those that occur in standard teacher-learner relationships—is notable because it made students' words and experiences part of the content and basis for learning. Encouraging students to listen to one another reinforced and demonstrated the value in their voices.

Similarly, Watson's aims for teaching *speaking* put students' needs at the center. She writes that these are the aims of teaching speaking:

I. To make the child realize the importance and worth of his own experiences.

II. To [support] the ability to use words and sentences accurately and vividly.

III. To extend the child's vocabulary and develop the [child's] ability to tell things in correct sequence.

IV. To [support] the ability to maintain prose and to use acceptable voice, articulation, and correct usage. ("Guidelines to Curriculum" 1)

Watson's aims put student needs at the center, further reinforcing the importance of starting with their knowledge and building confidence. If the Free School's purpose was to develop critical and active students, Watson knew that students first had to recognize that they could contribute in integrated public spaces outside of their home and church communities. Her consistent consciousness of students' worth directly opposed the rhetoric that had marked relationships between the white and Black communities in Prince Edward. Watson's suggestions for student-centered speaking activities continued to validate the importance of the learner's experiences:

I. Telling about pictures.

II. Telling about experiences—real or imagined.

III. Relaying messages; giving directions.

IV. Telling stories, jokes, or riddles.

V. Making informal conversation, introductions, announcements, or reports.

VI. Engaging in discussions, evaluating classroom activities—his [or her] own and others.

VII. Participating in choral speaking and dramatization. ("Guidelines to Curriculum" 2)

Almost all of these examples encourage students to compose content of their own for speeches rather than using material written by others. With students thus encouraged to speak in the dialect they spoke at home, the languages and literacies students came into the school with were valued. They also show flexibility in meeting the needs of students at varying levels of skill. Another important aspect of this approach for teachers was that it helped those who needed to gain their students' trust. Watson emphasized this point in a curriculum memo early in the Free School year: "Oral expression may be developed through well planned lessons that provide for active participation from the least able to the most able student" ("Curriculum Notes #11). This same memo reminds teachers of the importance of providing students time and space to talk and share their experiences about what they were learning, a practice she called "talk-time": "children need to do more talking and more listening to one another rather than to the teacher only" (Watson, "Curriculum Notes" #11). Teachers saw this technique of encouraging students to share their knowledge as central to the school's success. One language arts instructor wrote in a feedback form for the curriculum leader, "The technique or method of beginning each day with 'talk-time' has gradually caused each pupil to make a contribution as they talk about weather reports, news events, etc. This sets the stage for effective learning throughout the day (qtd. in "Curriculum Notes #11"). Talk-time not only provided a way to center student voices and experiences but also spoke to values from postwar education that expressed desires for students to have access to relevant information about the world around them.

Teacher evaluations also describe the inherent difficulty of working in the classroom with students who had had a wide range of experiences during the closures. For example, teacher reflections reveal that some struggled to follow the stories of children, who often blended real events with the imaginary or who relied heavily on folk wisdom and knowledge. As one teacher noted, "In observing a group of children, I realized that they had learned to substitute the unreal." This same teacher commented on what they recognized as a lack of trust in some students, who had difficulty adjusting to being back in school with so many teachers from outside the community: "They have become distrustful of outside existence" (qtd. in "Student Evaluation Reports" October 1963). The disposition of students factored heavily in daily work and in the relationships fostered with students. For some teachers, true empathy meant learning how to listen and present material in such a way as to encourage those who were uncomfortable.

Overall, however, teacher feedback forms suggest that speaking came easier to most students than writing and reading. For example, five evaluations from teachers across the lower unit in October 1963 included statements such as, "Speaking difficulties were largely a matter of fright. Children who find themselves not threatened and with a sympathetic ear to listen will start using in school those skills they use outside of school." Another teacher pointed out that speaking vocabularies were far ahead of reading or writing vocabularies: "I find that students are able to verbalize and use many words they cannot read." Teacher observations about reading education were more mixed. While one teacher wrote that "students read very little" since their schools had closed and that it had been difficult "to recapture" the skill as a consequence, another wrote, "They are so eager to learn to read that they are learning [it] fast." Writing skills were proving even more difficult. "Writing skills are returning painfully slowly," one teacher wrote. Another wrote that students "have had insufficient practice and training [in writing] . . . [such that students] write as they speak." "[N]ot many [students] have had a need to do any writing [since they left school four years ago]," another teacher noted. These complaints about dialect and the students' inability to write in a way deemed proficient by their teachers are of course typical of that time period, and similar observations continue to pervade conversations about linguistic ability and inferiority when students do not use Standard English. They also speak to the challenges that teachers themselves had to contend with as they established relationships with their students.

Watson had an answer for those teachers who felt they were plagued by this problem. Watson, citing educational consultant Dr. Beryl Parker, urges teachers to "free [themselves] and the children to talk, write, and dramatize spontaneously" ("Memo to Elementary Principals and Teachers"). She tasks teachers with acknowledging and removing their biases in order to develop good relationships with students. She acknowledges that teachers can have "barriers to overcome" if they are "to listen and look with sensitivity" ("Language for Self-Expression"). In other words, Watson called on teachers to put students' needs first and to reflect on their own practices. Her encouragement of teachers to not be bound by their expectations and to create space to hear the voices of all of their students reflects her commitment to acknowledging and respecting the agency of students. The approach used in the Free School classrooms was thus the antithesis of the treatment most Blacks received from the larger white Prince Edward community. The Free School approach was also reminiscent of the kind of treatment many Black students received in segregated schools before the closures. As the interviews in chapter 4 will demonstrate, and as previously discussed in chapter 1, while segregated schools often lacked physical resources, they made up for that deficiency with the type of care, concern, and inspiration the teachers shared with their students.

Watson's guidelines directly responded to claims that Black students were not capable. If the Free School's aim was to prepare students to be active citizens, then Watson's curriculum and guidance demonstrated her belief that students could become active citizens through rigorous course learning and an environment in which they as individuals and their community received respect.

James B. Cooley and His Vicars of the Democratic Tradition

James Cooley, principal of the Free School's upper unit, composed the high school statement of philosophy and oversaw the development of the curriculum. With forty-five faculty members to serve the upper unit students, Cooley, like Watson, needed to adapt Sullivan's policies to the lived experiences of his student population. Cooley's upper unit, which was affectionately called Robert Russa Moton High or Moton, after the all-Black high school the county had closed four years earlier, had the task of instructing a unique group of teenagers and young adults. Students who were sixteen or seventeen when the public schools closed were now in their early twenties. Some had left the county to work and came back when the opening of the Free School was announced, while others had started families, which made their attendance sporadic. In a feedback report, one teacher recounted that on the first day of school a student mentioned being as old as some of the teachers. Cooley's handbook and statement of philosophy exemplify localized practices attentive to the needs of these students. It listed policies and procedures central to running any high school but supplemented them with recognition of the unusual position of teachers and students (Cooley, "Prince Edward Moton Handbook").

Cooley's approach, like Watson's, was grounded in a commitment to demonstrating respect toward students, making student experiences part of the curriculum, and focusing on material that a traditional high school curriculum would provide. The Moton statement of philosophy, supplemental handbook, accreditation materials, and student newspaper attest to Cooley's commitment to making the upper unit responsive to the diverse needs of young adults. Cooley also had to decide whether to offer job training. The presence of adults intensified pressure to do so, and Cooley did forge a delicate balance between job training and college preparatory offerings. Jean Fairfax of the AFSC was a particularly strong advocate for vocational training, but Cooley saw such offerings as failing to fulfill the Free School's mission, a common tension in Black education. He did not want to educate students to enter the tobacco fields, the factories, or the homes of white families as they may have done during the closures. In keeping with this aim, Cooley and Sullivan filed a preliminary accreditation request with Virginia's Department of Education in January 1964, presenting the school's curriculum and seeking the power to grant high school diplomas. The application was approved, and the upper unit was authorized as a diploma-granting high school within the commonwealth. The request for accreditation would make visible to the entire state that this school and its students wanted to be recognized for the work they did in the classroom. This document would also demonstrate the type of learning that was occurring in this school, further seeking to disrupt the established ideas and stereotypes about what kinds of learning could and should take place among Black populations. The document outlined the types of courses offered and provided a description of the facilities, as well as the backgrounds of instructors.

Moton's statement of philosophy, a three-page document separate from the Moton handbook, begins with Cooley's call to teachers, staff, and administrators to serve as the true representatives of democracy: "The administration, faculty, and staff of Robert R. Moton High School of the Prince Edward Free School Association, as vicars of the Democratic Tradition, propose to set forth certain principles of philosophy upon which our program is to be maintained. First, we believe that all our students should be aware of their rights, responsibilities and roles as tenants of our democracy" ("Moton Philosophy" 1"). This was a bold proclamation; it figured the Free School as a direct challenge to segregation. Black students were named as deciders of their own roles—rather than depending on white counterparts to determine which rights they could responsibly hold. Cooley directly tied the Free School's educational aims to the goal of nurturing and building citizens. The religious connotation of the term "vicar" suggested a spiritual commitment to the stewardship of American democracy for teachers, staff, and administrators.

Cooley's educational philosophy for the Free School outlines ten outcomes for the upper unit, and it is a list heavily influenced by the National Education Association's (NEA) Cardinal Principles of Secondary Education. Recognizing the importance of high schools as integral for "social integration and building values," the NEA's 1918 Commission on the Reorganization of Secondary Education suggested a comprehensive school that would offer a variety of subjects, both vocational and college preparatory (*Cardinal Principles* 128). The commission's recommendations came from the context of a growing need to reorganize secondary schools to help better prepare students for entry into college and the work force.

Thematically, the beliefs behind Cooley's educational philosophy included having students understand their rights and responsibilities as US citizens; the importance of self-esteem; providing physical fitness and extracurricular activities, guidance, and support for students as they prepared for further academic pursuits and careers; and cultivating traits that would help them assume both family and work responsibilities. Each of these objectives was aimed to "develop the whole student body, mind, moral, spiritual, and aesthetic values" ("Moton Philosophy" 2). While Cooley's list relied heavily on the NEA's Cardinal Principles, there were additional objectives that were specific to the Free School.

Particular to the Free School was Cooley's view that grouping students by ability instead of age was necessary for academic success. In the language arts classes this proved integral. With some students coming into the school at fifteen or sixteen years of age and reading on a fourth- or fifth-grade level, they needed one-on-one tutoring to bring them to grade level. Students were placed in small groups in language arts classes with two or more teachers assigned to each group to allow for direct interaction. Much like the school-wide handbook, Cooley's brief philosophy statement again acknowledges the commitment to democracy: "We believe that all our students should be aware of their rights, responsibilities and roles as tenants of our democratic system" ("Moton Philosophy" 1). Apart from citizenship, the philosophy statement emphasized "self-worth" as a response to the degradation of Prince Edward's school closures. "We believe," the statement begins, "in the development of 'self.'" It described the role of others in this development: "By nurturing and encouraging 'self' development, we strive to create and maintain a climate of 'mutual respect' among students, parents, the administration, and faculty which should produce strong individuals who can meet the challenges of an ever-changing and interdependent world" ("Moton Philosophy" 1). Prioritizing teaching for self-development emphasized an awareness of the importance of aiding students in their journeys to become individuals, a practice that undergirded the Free School's philosophy.

Cooley articulates the desire to have students "meet the challenges" of an "ever-changing and interdependent world," further acknowledging the development of the individual as paramount for producing a population that could think independently and contribute to their communities. In this way, the curriculum had to speak to the needs of both individuals and the larger community and was a refutation of the notion that only Prince Edward's white community knew what was best for Blacks.

The philosophy statement closes by calling on the larger community to participate in the education of the students. Cooley's community-wide approach to education would have residents "practice sound principles of guidance which have their origin in the classroom"; it "encourages early vocational selection, and includes sympathetic, pupil-centered counseling aided by home, school, community and national resources" ("Moton Philosophy" 2).

Emphasizing the needs of the students and involving the entire community in efforts to help support them were integral to encouraging student development. The desire to involve the families of students encouraged a community effort toward education. Significantly, this approach figured the community as an aid; in spite of an alliance with the federal government and other monied interests, it did not figure a hierarchy that would place the school above the community. Monthly progress reports submitted to the board of trustees describe school events, which included choral concerts, plays, and assemblies, as moments to invite parents and friends to see students and teachers work.

Akin to Sullivan's opening letter with its acknowledgment of the "Herculean" effort teachers would need to put forth to face the school year, Cooley's statement of philosophy avowed the difficulty the school faced: "It is my hope that each of you will assume equal responsibility in all areas of operation. Our success will depend on the maximum cooperation of all teachers and will require concerted effort and a dedication to duty. We have accepted the challenge; let us prove we are equal to the task ahead" (Cooley, "Prince Edward Free School Association" [Moton Handbook]). To guide teachers, the handbook described a three-phase plan for lessons. The first phase, "Orientation," was intended "to stimulate interest and develop readiness for a school learning situation, and for readjustment in grouping." This phase gave teachers time to assess students' progress and make notes about who might need to be moved to another class. The second phase, "Basic Skills," consisted of "instruction [that] should be adjusted to ability levels of students with special emphasis on fundamental skills, health, study skills, and habits, school and social adjustment, until students are brought up to their normal grade level for their ages." This phase would look different in each class but was meant to provide students with the minimum ability needed for that particular course. In practice, students could move through classes quickly so that they might be able to cover more content in a year. The third phase, "Regular," was intended to prepare students to progress at their own pace: "Students should be grouped according to ability and placed in regular classes in which they follow the Virginia curriculum guides for their grade levels" (Cooley, "Prince Edward Free School Association" [Moton Handbook]). These levels and phases were meant to maximize instructional time and allow students agency and control in a variety of subjects.

There were two tracks available to students at this level: preparatory or terminal. The preparatory track was intended for those students who were college bound or going into an advanced training program after high school; the terminal program provided students with opportunities to take classes in home economics and automotive repair. The preparatory path required students to take a range of basic courses: English, mathematics, science (biology, chemistry, or physics), Virginia and US history, world history and geography, physical education, additional units selected from specified programs, and electives ("Requirements for Graduation" 3). Electives included a range of course options: foreign language, music, agriculture, industrial education, home economics, art, and commercial subjects. By allowing students to plot their own course of study and choose between a preparatory and a vocational track, the school respected their own understanding of their interests and needs and replicated the offerings that would have been available at a traditional public school. Mirroring the normal public school system gave students an opportunity to attend schools that they had been deprived of for four years and to further their education. The Free School approach ultimately offered testimony to what Black (and white) children were able to do together.

Connecting Textbooks and Real World Experiences

Giving students ample opportunity to practice literacy skills was certainly not limited to the classroom. The Moton handbook called on homeroom teachers to "organize homerooms with officers or student leaders to plan activities which will meet the interest and needs of members." The homeroom period, a daily meeting time, was an extension of classroom learning as students practiced their rhetorical skills by arranging "panel discussions, student debates and other discussions" (Cooley, "Prince Edward Free School Association" [Moton Handbook]). Free School teachers encouraged students to use language and participate in a variety of discourses for different purposes.

Extracurricular activities, according to the handbook, were "an integral part of the high school program" (Cooley, "Prince Edward Free School Association" [Moton Handbook]). Students could play basketball or baseball, run track, work on the student newspaper, and serve in the student government association. There were also opportunities in the fine arts, such as a creative dance group, drama club, and choral society. The Future Black Leaders of America and the student council reflected the school's mission of training citizens. Sullivan's memoir reflected his understanding of the importance of these offerings: "To meet the needs of so diverse a student body, and to hold those students who might be discouraged by the seemingly monumental odds against them, the Moton faculty kept activities going at full tilt until five-thirty each afternoon and on Saturdays too. The library and science labs, the art and music rooms, all stayed open" (*Bound* 120). Diverse extracurricular activities and extended operating times helped to meet the core curricular goals of developing students' ability to think and express their thoughts as citizens of their school community. Extracurricular opportunities to read, speak, study, and use language provided students a chance to practice in diverse spaces outside of the typical constraints found in traditional classrooms. This also supported the school's mission of education for the whole student.

The student council consisted of a group of elected student representatives. They were charged with drafting a set of guidelines for school-sponsored activities. Sullivan describes the students' self-governance as being unique for the time period, given that secondary-school student government associations were usually created by teachers and administrators: "At the same time, a student council, elected by the students themselves, was given the responsibility for drafting ground rules covering all activities. Their rules were more rigid than I had expected, and I was pleasantly surprised at the positive reaction of the student body to the code of conduct established by their peers. Especially encouraging was the continued attendance of the older [students]" (Sullivan, *Bound* 120–21). Students were allowed to develop their own rules for governance, which allowed them to put the school's mission into practice. As agents in this space, they created rules, negotiated with teachers and administrators, and enacted the change they envisioned.

Archival artifacts suggest that developing supporting programs for Moton was not an easy endeavor. Jean Fairfax wrote a letter to each member of the board of trustees in October 1963 suggesting a special program targeted at the older youth returning to the classroom. In this letter, Fairfax outlined the concerns she and her group had for the older students: "I do not believe they will come to school and stay unless a special program with job-training is planned for them. However, I doubt that the kind of program which would be adequate will get off the ground soon. I believe that a good vocational counseling project located wherever one can find these young people would give them the incentive to return to school. Perhaps a special basic education course could be set up for them with a pre-vocational emphasis while plans are being developed for the training program" (Fairfax, Letter).

One way to engage with this issue was to make jobs in the high school available to students. A program that resembled later work-study programs allowed students to work and receive payment for their services as bus drivers, library aides, or secretaries while also attending school, which also gave these students a sense of shared ownership of the school. While traditional public schools certainly had vocational programs that allowed students to get experience in particular fields, they were not paying students wages for engaging in that work. Sullivan described Cooley's program as one that recognized the participants as adults: "Jim Cooley made them responsible for their own actions; he also gave them an opportunity to earn spending money (and self-respect) as cafeteria workers, library assistants or playground supervisors. They became first-class citizens almost overnight because they were treated as the adults they were" (*Bound* 121). Cooley's program reflected his understanding of his students' position as young Black people in the rural South. The development of this work-study arrangement was a creative endeavor designed to support students' need to work, to encourage them to resume their education, and to recognize them as the adults that many were.

Students also found opportunities to show their agency through more traditional means, such as the upper unit newspaper. That publication, the *Moton Ea-*

gle, encouraged student-directed self-expression. Jay P. Childers's central claim in *The Evolving Citizen: American Youth and the Changing Norms of Democratic Engagement* is crucial to understanding the importance of Moton's student newspaper. Childers works from the premise that "the norms of democratic citizenship evolve over time as the social and cultural norms of a society change." For adolescents, Childers argues, "the process of learning democratic citizenship present[s] a particularly salient opportunity to better understand these changing norms" (4). For Childers, one way to examine these changes is through high school newspapers, and his findings represent the changes in civic participation over a span of just forty-five years (1965–2010). His analysis demonstrates the importance of looking to student-run media for a better understanding of how adolescents understand democracy, democratic participation, and their role or roles in it. Certainly, for Free School students in the upper unit, their newspaper served as a space for them to exercise their voices and take on issues of importance to them, such as the school closures.

The Free School archive holds several issues of the *Moton Eagle*. One issue, dated Monday, February 17, 1964, was a mixture of both serious news topics and lighthearted coverage of entertainment and social happenings. A running column called "The Students Speak" invited students to respond to what *Eagle* staff described as a "controversial subject," in this case, "Should girls be allowed to wear slacks to basketball games?" The responses reflected the times, as all students agreed that slacks were not "lady like" and were even "a disgrace" to the school. However passé the sentiments, the column reflected students' level of comfort in expressing themselves. An unsigned editorial titled "What about School in 64–65?" narrates the history of the school closures and provides important details on that history. The author calls on readers to think of Prince Edward's original role in the *Brown* case, recounts the role of the Supreme Court, and asks how it was possible that the schools had not reopened, even with *Brown* ten years in the past. The editorial emphasizes the importance of reopening the schools to students who might have the opportunity graduate, and it states, sagely, "Let us all hope that the people concerned will make their responsibility the best possible education for us all." This editorial showcases what is likely to be one student's astute analysis of the crisis. On behalf of the students, it connects education and democracy, highlighting both as an issue of importance for all the county's citizens, not just the Black community. While a larger number of issues would provide a greater sense of the newspaper's scope, based on this single run of the newspaper it seems possible to conclude that the *Moton Eagle* provided students with a public forum in which to respond to the world around them. That they took it, with seriousness and ambition, reflects the pedagogy that encouraged teachers to listen and provide support, rather than implementing a liberatory agenda from the top down.

An issue dated March 26, 1964, included a similar balance, again presenting both fun and serious inquiry. A report on the young woman selected to be Miss Moton 1964 made the front-page headline, while an editorial on how student actions were representative of Moton was the leading editorial. In this short piece, titled "Is Moton the Best by Your Action?," the author tasks students with being representatives of their school and showing school pride both inside and outside of the halls of Moton: "It's the best—that's what we all seek in and out of school. Students, to make sure that MHS is the best, we should participate in activities, cooperate with each other, and try to keep MHS tops in the public eye in and out of school." This appeal to make sure that students were on their best behavior as a matter of showing school spirit was aimed at boosting student attendance at both games and daily classes. Students were reminded that "actions speak louder than a lusty yell. Start showing concern. Your cleanliness, orderliness, consideration, cooperation in and around school reveals your school spirit, pride, and interest in MHS" (2). Such an appeal speaks to students' recognition that they were representatives of their school. Certainly many schools teach students that they are representatives of their institutions, but in this particular case it would seem that students felt they were even more in the public eye. This same issue contained a report on the Library Club's visit to nearby Longwood University Library and a book review on *Lord of the Flies*.

In addition to engaging in these more traditional school practices developed to help prepare them for active lives as citizens, students in the upper school were eager to participate in what could be seen as a pinnacle of citizenship: voter registration. While I did not find evidence regarding this initiative in the Free School archive, Sullivan provided a positive account of the students' desire to sponsor a voter registration drive: "Then there was the matter of voting rights. A group of our high school students asked if they could assist in a voter registration drive. For a period of six weeks, with the help of an interested staff, some twenty-four young people from the Free School spent all their spare time traveling to a remote section of the county and preparing prospective voters for registration. As a result, over two hundred persons were added to the voter rolls of Prince Edward County" (*Bound* 204). Interestingly, in Sullivan's own reflection of student success in this endeavor, he mentions two principles that also made the Free School a success: first, the students knew the community they were working with, and second, they were committed to the work (204). The dedication and understanding students used as they worked to register voters in their community mirrored the respect and commitment of their Free School teachers. I cannot ascertain whether students modeled their voter registration program after their own teachers' pedagogical approaches. I do believe, however, that the students' desire to participate in the voter registration drive *and* their request for permission and assistance from staff demonstrated the students' awareness of the school's desire to make training and preparation for citizenship a lived practice.

The Free School was a multilayered response to the school closures in Prince Edward. The reality of the school was that it took four years until the government offered a response, which meant that a number of children went almost half a decade without formal schooling. The Free School was a necessary response, but it is impossible to recoup four years' worth of formal education in the space of nine months. The mission of the school was to provide its students with a program that would help prepare them to be engaged citizens, and administrators focused on literacy as the way to achieve this goal. Still, there were competing perspectives from government leaders and school administration on how that mission would be realized. With students coming in with such a wide range of experiences and expectations, there was no one-size-fits all approach to doing the work necessary in classrooms. While the use of nongraded classrooms and team teaching allowed for students to have more attention and direct instruction when necessary, the attitudes of teachers also proved to be integral to meeting the goals of the school. Teachers had to position themselves in such a way as to both bear witness to the knowledge and expressions of their students and to gain their trust so that students would be receptive to what they had to teach. Archival documents demonstrate how the school positioned itself in the community as a response to arguments about integrated learning and citizenship preparation, but documents can tell only part of the story. An important perspective on the school is available through the words of Free School students, the subject of the next chapter.

4

Free School Students Speak

I am glad to see the teachers working together, both white and colored. And I
hope it show the people in Prince Edward County that Negros and whites can
get along, even in working for a common cause.

ANONYMOUS MOTON HIGH SCHOOL STUDENT, OCTOBER 1963

They did, I really believe, the best they could do. . . . Lots of people complain
about this and complain about that, but it was a lot that had to be done to pull
everybody back.

REV. EVERETT BERRYMAN, AUGUST 2012

Stories of the civil rights movement are often told with adults as the primary
agents of change; however, young people made a large impact on the movement's
process and were, in many situations, on the front lines. From Ruby Bridges, the
first black student to integrate an elementary school in the South, to the Children's Crusade of 1963, in which more than one thousand Black students skipped
school to march in downtown Birmingham, ultimately leading to the desegregation of stores there, for young people the battlegrounds included both the streets
and the classrooms. If the Free School was a response to white supremacy, then
the civil rights work of students was an outgrowth of the Free School's challenge
to the status quo.

While the Free School's institutional response to racism had multiple audiences, students were in the middle. This chapter presents and analyzes the
observations and reflections of Free School students in two ways. First, I present the experiences of students as reported by teachers in evaluation reaction
reports and as recounted in Neil Sullivan's memoir. Second, I present reflections

directly from former students captured from interviews I conducted. The objective of this chapter is to examine the dimensions of the education students received at the Free School and to explore how they understood the Free School's message.

During the academic year, teachers completed what were called "Student Evaluation: A Reaction Report" forms in October and November 1963, and a summation survey in May 1964. The forms, generated from Sullivan's office, asked for a range of information about classroom activities, student behavior, and teacher supply needs. Evaluations from October and November allowed for narrative responses, and most teachers submitted the forms anonymously. The end-of-the-year evaluations used a survey format and asked teachers to agree or disagree with statements. Certainly the evaluations served a particular rhetorical purpose. Teachers were reporting to their supervisors about that which they were being paid to do, and so there was hierarchy and job security at stake. However, the forms were anonymous for the most part, and that seemed to provide some level of comfort with regard to what teachers reported. As this chapter will describe, themes that surfaced among these fragments suggest the reliability of what teachers reported about student experiences.

Student Concerns through the Eyes of Teachers

In a brief note to teachers at the top of each report, Sullivan describes the documents as a means of "gathering material" and explains their importance in the process of programmatic assessment: "Documentation of student attitude is necessary if proper evaluation is to be made of the four-year closing of public schools in Prince Edward County." Sullivan recognized the need to collect data that could capture student and teacher experiences. Given the questions listed, the reports appear to serve two functions. First, the October report was focused primarily on collecting data about how students were adjusting to being back in school, perhaps as a way to mark or trace the gravity of the situation. Second, the reports from November included questions that encouraged teachers to reflect on the nongraded and team-teaching approach and to better understand how the students were receiving the curriculum and pedagogical approaches being used.

The questions from the October reports asked for more reporting than reflection. They sought to gain more information about early student experiences and reactions to being in the classroom and unexpected occurrences. The questions asked were as follows:

1. What was the most unusual incident (including a child or group of children) which you observed during the first three weeks of school?

2. What student reaction (a statement made by a child) was the most unusual? This should be in relation to school or his assignment.

3. What student attitude was most unusual?

4. What was the most amusing statement made by a child resulting from his absence during a four-year period?

5. What was the most pathetic statement made by a child?

6. In your opinion, what has been the handicap to a child denied formal education? Please list in order, giving number 1 highest priority.

7. What, in your opinion, will help eliminate student absenteeism? ("Student Evaluation Reports," October 1963)

Several themes were present across the reports of student responses that teachers captured. First, students spoke about the hindrance of being out of school for four years. Second, many students expressed their lack of trust in schools and authority figures. Finally, students displayed their own understandings of citizenship, which the teachers recounted. Most prevalent across this first set of evaluations were teachers' reports that students were very vocal about their frustration at being behind. Before moving further in the evaluations, I would like to briefly return to the climate of public schools before the closures. This context helps to explain the student reactions expressed in both the archival materials and the interviews.

Prior to the closures in 1959, the segregated schools in Prince Edward may have lacked resources, but they received a great deal of support from the Black community. Kara Miles Turner enumerates the many ways Black parents offered support for Black education in her "'Liberating Lifescripts': Prince Edward County, Virginia, and the Roots of *Brown v. Board of Education*." Turner's description recounts how parents paid for private transportation to and from school, organized funds to build the county's Black high school, and supplemented teacher salaries out of their own pockets (90). As reflections from former students will elucidate, Black teachers working in the segregated schools were often very dedicated to student learning. After the closures, many students ended their tenure with public schools, having had good experiences in classrooms. As discussed in chapter 2, students had a range of learning experiences during the closure period. Some students continued their educations outside of the county, while others received instruction from their parents or older siblings at home, and there was thus no standard in terms of what to expect of students' abilities. Most prevalent across this first set of evaluations were teacher reports of students' frustration at their lack of academic skills through no fault of their own.

One teacher described a student's physical reaction to being illiterate: "The most unusual incident I have observed occurred in a seventh-grade room I was visiting. A 14-year-old girl got sick to her stomach because she doesn't know how to read." Another teacher recalled, "A twelve-year-old boy burst into tears saying he did not want to read from a primer because that was 'Kid stuff,' yet he was incapable of reading from any other book." Others bemoaned their prolonged absence from the classroom: "I wish I was six years old instead of being ten and just entering school" ("Student Evaluation Reports," October 1963). These children's responses suggest the pain and embarrassment inflicted on them as a result of the closures.

Like the twelve-year-old who didn't want to read from the primer, another student "who could not write his name in a legible manner objected to his lessons in penmanship[,] saying they were for children" ("Student Evaluation Reports," October 1963). Teachers had to contend with varied scholastic abilities as well as the students' own frustrations about their academic progress. The ungraded system that grouped students according to age and allowed them to move across levels depending on their ability accelerated some of these resentments. A drawback of the ungraded system was that older students found themselves placed alongside those much younger, which would have made it easier to conclude that needed lessons were an affront to a student's maturity. Christopher Bonastia's work on the closure period presents interviews from three former Free School students who were critical of the Free School's impact. For these former students, the nongraded structure caused more angst than good. Bonastia cites the example of John Hurt's explanation: "You sat down, and the other kids be turning in their work . . . [and] you had got as far as putting your name on your paper. . . . I mean, you're sitting up in school, you got a first grade reading level, and you're sitting up in eighth grade, people doing eighth, ninth grade work, you know" (qtd. in Bonastia 157). For other students it was difficult to come to the Free School after having been in school outside of the county. Bonastia's interview with Rita Mosely, who had been out of the county in another school system, demonstrates the issue of transferring. She shared this view: "It was very confusing. It was kids like myself that had gone away to school for a few years. There were kids that had not gone to school the whole four years. . . . So all of us was together. And the people that were here were trying to place us, trying [to] figure out what to do with us. I personally feel that I would have been better off if I had not come back to Free School, if I had stayed where I was and continued in the academic curriculum that I was in" (qtd. Bonastia 157). There was no way that a temporary, one-year school could address the needs of all of its students who had had education withheld from them for four years.

Teacher reflections certainly capture these frustrations, but they also report the excitement from students about being in an academic space once more. One teacher quoted a student as saying, "I am back in school, give me work, more work in order to catch up for lost time" and several who said simply, "I want to learn" ("Student Evaluation Reports," October 1963). Likewise, Sullivan reflects on the decision to keep some of the school resources available for more of the day because the desire of students to stay at school was so strong: "To meet the needs of so diverse a student body, and to hold those students who might be discouraged by the seemingly monumental odds against them, the Moton faculty kept activities going at full tilt until five-thirty each afternoon and on Saturdays, too. The library and science labs, the art and music rooms, all stayed open" (Sullivan, *Bound* 120). Extended day programs and after-school activities responded to the students' need to have additional access to teachers, supplies, and equipment for their use. Thus, these reports speak back to the narrative that Blacks lacked the desire and initiative to learn. The provision of extra time for extracurricular activities and the use of class space allowed for community building and offered a sanctuary for students who had been without access to such spaces for four years.

As the Free School expressed its mission to provide students with skills that were designed to help prepare them for citizenship roles, of note are the teacher responses in the October reports that describe what students were saying and thinking about citizenship and democracy. One teacher noted that a student commented, "I guess President Kennedy saw that the Peace Corp. is needed more in Farmville than overseas." This statement shows both an understanding that the federal government had neglected to act on behalf of the Black community for four years and that the need was dire, a need such as might be found in a third world community. Similarly, as the statement in the epigraph shows, another teacher reported that some students were aware of the importance of the efforts being made to demonstrate the importance of integration: "I am glad to see the teachers working together, both white and colored. And I hope it show the people in Prince Edward County that Negros and whites can get along, even in working together for a common cause." This young person's statement acknowledges the impact of the integrated staff on both students and the greater community. He or she understood the integration of the staff as an important step toward change in the Prince Edward community. A third instance suggests the sophisticated understanding of students at the Free School: "During the first opening devotions of a class period a girl raised her hand saying she did not want to sing patriotic songs, and asked to sing her song. Then she led 'Jesus Keep Me Near the Cross,' and afterward, prayed of her own free will. This incident happened on the first morning only." Choosing to sing a hymn over a patriotic song suggests a primary allegiance not to country but to her religion, unsurprising in an environment that expressed an investment in faith traditions. Whether the student joined in singing the patriotic songs on subsequent days after the single display of dissent on the momentous day of the school's opening felt like enough or because the Free School made her feel more invested in America is unknown. The incident suggests that some students were aware of their roles as citizens and the right to self-expression no matter what white supremacist ideology purported. The teacher who reported this incident does not reflect on it, but given the atmosphere of respect for students cultivated at the Free School, it seems likely that he or she understood the sense of betrayal that may have prompted this event. Another teacher reported that one of the most unusual things in the classroom was "three students' refusal to salute the flag" ("Student Evaluation Reports," October 1963). Like the reaction of the young woman who sang a hymn rather than patriotic songs, perhaps this was an act of resistance to what the students felt as forced democratic participation.

Practices of citizenship were not absent in the Black community. Even with the schools closed, students would have seen displays of citizenship before entering the Free School year. From home to the church, many of the Free School students saw displays of citizenship in family members working for voting rights, and through church sermons that preached on the Gospels with a focus on social justice for the poor and marginalized, and conversations about mobilizing efforts for better public school opportunities. Most Free School students came into the school year with knowledge of what it meant to be a Black citizen in Prince Edward. Many understood schooling and education to be a vehicle by which they too could gain skills needed for citizenship practice. The reflections of some teachers further demonstrate that many students fully recognized the connection between school attendance and citizenship: "A student stated that the closing of schools had hindered him from getting his education as early as he should have and therefore had delayed his opportunity for becoming a good citizen of the U.S." This student's comment exhibited an awareness that school is supposed to serve as a site for teaching civic behaviors and the skills necessary for participation in a democracy and that the closures withheld that from him. In another comment, a teacher reported, "A student told me Virginia rejoined the Union when the schools were reopening in Prince Edward County" ("Student Evaluation Reports," October 1963). This student's response invokes the secession that prompted the Civil War and the notion of American democracy as hinging on a commitment to public education.

The November reports strike a balance between asking teachers to reflect on the students' reactions to the school—now two months into the academic year—

and on the pedagogical methods they were using. The prompting questions included the following:

1. What personality change, if any, have you noted in the children after seven weeks of school?

2. Which teaching device or technique brought out the best in each child?

3. Attendance has definitely improved, but I am still not satisfied. How, in your opinion, can we improve attendance?

4. Which of the communication skills seems most difficult for the children to recapture? (Reading/Writing/Speaking). Why?

5. Please describe the decorum of the student body over the first seven weeks of the school year.

6. What is the student reaction to small group instruction?

7. What is the student reaction to large group instruction?

8. Flexibility is one of the advantages of the non-graded school. When a child makes unusual progress and moves ahead of his group he should be reassigned. Have you observed any such progress and how do you handle the situation?

9. What do you do when the reverse of [number] eight above occurs?

10. Has anything unusual occurred in student reaction or behavior which surprised you? (Student Evaluation Reports, November 1963)

The responses to these questions contain fewer remarks about citizenship, as they focus more on teaching techniques. Most teachers had overwhelmingly positive things to say about how students were adjusting after having seven full weeks to learn more about their teachers and to form connections with other students. Teachers consistently reported that students were "relaxed" and "at ease":

The children seem more sure of themselves.

Students seem to have a sense of composure and security; they are at ease with teachers and fellow students.

The children appear to be more relaxed and happy. Shyness is disappearing. They speak more freely. (Student Evaluation Reports, November 1963)

Trust and student comfort are issues in every educational setting, but here, with some students expressing apprehensiveness about their attendance, the fact that some were finding their stride suggests that teachers were making an effort to make these spaces feel safe. A lower unit teacher, who self-identified as Mrs. Pena, gets at her own recognition of the role time played in having students come to trust and express care for their teachers. She noted, "There is a general relaxation of tenseness, of fright, children are finding friends, becoming adjusted. The students seem to understand better the love and understanding I try to give them." Later in her report, she indicates that, to remedy the problem of absenteeism, teachers should work even harder to make school a positive experience: "Make school a more pleasant place to be for the child. Less red lettered POOR on written assignments of students who can't write and couldn't possibly understand the words on those mimeographed papers they have to finish and fill in for homework or classwork or whatever" (Student Evaluation Reports, November 1963). Teachers such as this one were acutely aware of the ways in which this group of students needed to be reminded that school could be a good experience in spite of the difficulties they faced with coming in behind where they would have been had the schools not been closed. The need to build students' confidence and comfort in school was just as important as the academic skills they were being taught. Initiating a shift in students' attitudes so that they felt more assured and confident would also help student academic performance. Giving attention to building relationships with students where teachers were respectful and exhibited care and concern was also a necessary step in terms of citizenship instruction. Teachers needed to allow students an opportunity to feel welcomed and supported, to demonstrate to them that they were valued, to allow them to feel comfortable in using their voices.

A teacher from the lower unit who self-identified on the report as Mr. Cuffee suggested that the students' more positive attitudes had a direct influence on their ability to work: "The students appear to be leveling off into normal adolescents with their energies directed into normal, constructive channels. They appear to be less defiant since they now have schools. They have rediscovered the thrill of adolescent peer groups in school without having to assume the roles of adults within the confines of a hostile community." Many of the students in the upper unit came into the Free School with a most unique set of experiences. Some of the older students worked on their families' farms or had to care for younger siblings during the closure period. A reflection from Mrs. Barnes, an elementary school English teacher, also seems to suggest that spending more time in school allowed students to feel confident enough to ask for help when they needed it, which also helped their progress: "They are more relaxed and at ease in school. Also, they are now not afraid to admit it when they don't know something." Another elementary school teacher, Madge Shipp, also spoke to the students' ability to feel more at ease with participating in classroom activities after having been back in school for a while: "The pupils were shy at first. The children seem to have a feeling of self-confidence now. They readily take part in discussions or answer questions in complete statements" (Student Evaluation Reports, November 1963). All of this suggests that time was key in having students get acclimated to their new school. The first priority for teachers was building relationships and community. For students who may have been uneasy with the transition back into school, establishing these relationships was paramount for learning and for sharing their emerging expressions of citizenship.

These teacher viewpoints are not unexpected; with students having more time to create a community, adjust to being in a school environment, and getting to know their teachers, there would naturally be an improved atmosphere in the classroom. The reflections teachers were able to capture help us to understand just a bit how the students reacted to the Free School endeavor. While it was certainly not a one-size-fits-all solution to the many issues that students faced, it did provide an alternative statement about who was willing to respond to the needs of a community that had persisted despite having no access to public education. The teachers' reports detail the range of emotions studies held: frustration, fear, resentment, cautious optimism, hope, and excitement. There is no one way to capture all of the experiences of the students from the archives, but interviews do put the themes mined from the archive into conversation with contemporary reflections from former students.

Former Free School Students Looking Back and Move Forward

I interviewed seven former Free School students. All seven of the interviewees were unable to attend school because of the closures. From the seven, only five recollected their time during the Free School year. Appearing in this chapter are portions of the interviews of five of those persons: Rev. Everett Berryman, Shirley Earley, Clara Johnson, Armstead "Chuckie" Reid, and Bernetta Watkins. All resided in Prince Edward County prior to the school closings in 1959. As I demonstrated in chapters 1 and 2, whites in power had control of the narrative about the Black community, and the primary purpose of that narrative was maintaining the power structure in Prince Edward and marginalizing the perspectives from the Black community. In the section that follows, I seek to bring the stories and experiences expressed by students to the center. That is, rather than use the interview responses as a way to reinforce themes from the archive, I present them as a way to read and understand the themes found in the archive anew. These themes, demonstrating respect for students, a standard literacy education that welcomed students' individual expressions of language and identity, and pedagogical practices that supported and encouraged a variety of ways for students to practice civic participation, were crafted as a response to the community's unique needs. Through these interviews, I seek to understand how these students, albeit a small group, received this message about literacy, race, and respect. In crafting questions for the interviews, I sought information about the students' experiences prior to as well as during their year in the Free School. I begin with a brief biographical sketch for each. Their experiences in school before the closures provided important background and context for how they experienced their Free School year.

Rev. Everett Berryman Jr. was born and raised in the western area of Prince Edward County, a region known as Pamplin. Reverend Berryman grew up on his family's farm and enjoyed attending school before the closures, citing good experiences with teachers, who were like family. Farm living would also provide him with a different set of experiences with regard to interacting with white people. Living in the more rural area of the county meant that both Blacks and whites often shared resources and labor. Berryman was quick to draw a firm distinction about this: "Now, mind you again, the laws said we couldn't eat in the same restaurant, the laws said we couldn't intermarry between the races, the laws said I can't go to the theater, I can't drink out of the same water fountain. . . . In the country we had to rely on each other to get in the crops, to plant the crops, to do this and the other. One person couldn't do all of that."

Still, one of the largest impacts of segregationist control came into Reverend Berryman's life after his sixth-grade year, when the schools were first closed. During the closures, he would attend the training centers organized by PECCA to help students keep skills fresh. His own mother, Cula Berryman, helped to run one of the training centers. Eventually his family would relocate to Appomattox County for a short period of time so that he and his siblings could continue their schooling. Berryman recalled the shock he felt when he first learned the schools were closed: "[A]s a child we thought, 'You can't close school! How do schools just not open?'" Reflecting on the perspective he had as an eleven-year-old, Berryman admitted that there was some excitement about the schools being closed at first, because he was thinking it meant an "extended summer." That excitement would soon give way to frustration once he realized that he was falling behind. Reverend Berryman would return to Prince Edward and attend the full Free School year and go on to graduate from Moton High School. After high school, he served in the Navy and then went on to receive a bachelor's degree in education from Virginia Seminary and College, now known as Virginia University of Lynchburg.

Bernetta Stiff Watkins was six when the schools first closed in Prince Edward. Growing up in Prince Edward, she came from a family that had been actively involved in the fight for better educational opportunities in the county. She credits her uncle and grandfather in particular for fighting to provide bus transportation for the segregated schools prior to the closures. Coming from a family determined to persevere on its own, Watkins would reflect that her family members were the kind of people who were "not going to lick anybody's feet, toes, or anything else. We'll struggle to have our own and not be holding to anybody." During the closure period, Watkins spent most of her time at home, as her family refused to break itself up by sending the children away in spite of offers to have them live in other counties to attend school. Her family also needed the assistance of the children to help with the farm. She would recall going to a teacher's nearby home to do some math and reading work at night.

Watkins looked forward to her Free School year with great anticipation: "I don't remember how I heard about it. I remember anticipating and getting ready and being excited." While she was anxious for the schools to reopen, her family was skeptical: "It was like each year, no we were not going to do anything we were just going to hang tight because the next year they [schools] will open, and the next year they will open, and the next year they will open, until you woke up and it was four years later." Her Free School year would mark her first-ever full year of school. Watkins would go on to graduate near the top of her class in high school and would earn a bachelor's degree in history from Norfolk State University in Norfolk, Virginia. She returned to Prince Edward and found employment as a social worker.

Clara Johnson was eleven and in the fifth grade when the schools closed in 1959. She was the youngest child in her family, and her mother was a major proponent of education for all of her children. During the first year of the closure, her mother would encourage the children to do schoolwork at home and help one another. In the second year, Johnson's mother sent them to nearby Cumberland County schools through an arrangement she had with a friend who lived there. Johnson and her siblings would walk the children to and from school while her mother's friend worked the night shift at a nearby hospital. In the morning, all of the kids would go to school. They were able to keep this up until the Christmas break, when Cumberland County informed them that they would have to pay tuition to continue attending school there. Because her family could not afford the tuition, Johnson and her siblings would lose another year of school. In the third year, Johnson and her siblings were sent to Norwalk, Connecticut, to live with an older sibling who had married and relocated there. Her mother also had a friend in Stanford, Connecticut, who invited some of Johnson's siblings to come and live with her as well. Although Johnson was happy to be in school, she was also homesick.

Returning to Prince Edward in the summer of 1963, Johnson would be back in time for the sit-ins and protests that would erupt across Farmville that summer. She remembers telling her mother that she was going to participate in the College Shoppe sit-in, for which she would be sent to jail. Johnson recalls telling her mother, "[Y]ou know, Mom, this is going to impact our family life," to which her mother responded that she should do "whatever you think you need to do." Johnson would go on to continue her education at Prince Edward County High School after the Free School year.

Armstead D. "Chuckie" Reid was eight years old in 1959. Born and raised in Farmville, Reid was the youngest of his siblings. He admits that he was so young he did not always know what was happening with the school closures, but he remembers attending the crash courses at the local churches. In spite of his young age, he did remember thinking that it was strange that the friends he had had in school were no longer around: "I'm thinking we thought maybe it would be like that for a couple of days, but as time went on, and on, and on, you start wondering what's happening with the friends that we had." Reid grew up close to the town's center with lots of other families around. In addition to remembering the crash programs, he recalls doing "playschool" in the afternoon with friends. During their free time, Reid and his friends would "play and draw" and utilize the help of crash program teachers in their endeavors. Reid would attend the Free School year and continue his education in the public schools once they reopened.

While education was important, Reid had another "classroom" he enjoyed spending time in: First Baptist Church, which was his home church and the church of Reverend Griffin. Reid remembers it as being the hub for activity and organizing; it was also one of the places where he realized that he wanted to do something for his community. Reid's interest in public service would be manifest in many ways. With a group of his peers and under the tutelage of Reverend Griffin, he would help to run a local newsletter, *The Voice: A Newsletter Published by and for the Concerned Citizens of Prince Edward County, Virginia*. The newsletter would carry stories about local politics and issues of concern to the Black community. Later, Reid would be elected to serve as a town council representative for his ward (Race Street, Griffin Boulevard, and Hill Streets). In 2013, he was elected as Farmville's first Black vice-mayor.

Shirley Nunnally Earley was born in Rice, an area in Prince Edward just west of the county seat, Farmville. She had just completed second grade at High Rock School, a one-room school, in Rice when the public schools closed. Her school experiences before the closures were overwhelmingly positive. She recalls being invited to her teacher's home for lunch and being impressed with her teacher's ability to teach across a variety of courses and to play the piano and sing after work was done. Earley's parents farmed tobacco for a living. As reflected in the stories from Reverend Berryman and Clara Johnson, initially Shirley Earley understood the closures as an extended break, but that was quickly challenged once she realized that others were going to school. "[E]ven at that age . . . [I knew] that something wasn't right about this," she said.

Her own mother would work diligently to help her children maintain and expand skills at home. Earley recalls her mother working with them on cursive, telling time, multiplication, and reading. When Earley attended the Free School, she was excited to be back in school with kids from all over the county. She would continue her education in Prince Edward once the schools reopened. Her love of being in the classroom and learning, as well as her mother's dedication to education, would lead her to continue her own education and become a social studies teacher and later a guidance counselor in nearby Nottoway County.

While the experiences of each of the interviewees varied, there were several similarities that emerged across the stories they shared. Each of the former students described positive experiences in segregated schools before the closures, in spite of those schools' limited resources. For each of them, the tenacity of their families during the closure period helped them to have access to learning and educational opportunities. If their parents were unable to teach them, they worked to find resources and people who could. Finally, while they had very positive feelings about their year at the Free School, they also recognized that it had not and could not have solved the problems the school closures had created.

Reflections on Prince Edward County Schools before the Closures

The experiences of Free School students during the closures were varied: some were in school, while others had yet to officially begin because of age requirements. What remained consistent across the responses of those who had been in school was the fondness they expressed when they recalled their school experiences.

Reverend Berryman was eleven and a student at Mary E. Branch Elementary School No. 1 in Farmville when the public schools closed. He recalled the years before the school closures fondly: "We had very educated teachers and they knew how to structure us so that we could learn in the process of having fun. We had teachers who were teaching and who were concerned about our general welfare. The teachers were almost like parents." This connection to the teachers and identification of them as being extended family was reminiscent of the experiences in many segregated schools. Teachers were held in high regard in the Black community. While many segregated schools lacked resources, the teachers often went above and beyond to show students that they cared and were committed to their success in spite of a hostile world that said otherwise (Foster xiii; Walker 3). For

Berryman, school was a place that provided both a challenging and a nurturing environment: "We just enjoyed going to school."

Clara Johnson also described her experience as pleasant: "My school experience was good." She described teachers who were smart, competent, and caring: "I always liked school and I think we had a trove of really wonderful teachers who taught us a lot. We learned with them. They were all Black teachers, but I found out later in life that they prepared us. We weren't just a generation from Prince Edward who didn't learn anything. I found out later when I went to school in the North that we knew a lot. We were ahead of them in some aspects." Her recollection of the intelligence of her teachers was not an anomaly. In many instances, Black teachers had just as much education as their white counterparts even though they were consistently thought to be inferior to white educators (Foster xxix). Historical accounts suggest that other Black schoolchildren had similar experiences during this time period. While schools in Black communities had poor resources in terms of both facilities and materials, their teachers were often extremely dedicated. They knew the difficult road their students faced and were determined to prepare them to disprove hateful stereotypes. Adam Fairclough's *A Class of Their Own: Black Teachers in the Segregated South* describes the importance of teachers in the Black community. Fairclough writes, "Their dogged pursuit of better schools reflected a conviction of their own work and the work of their students" (390). Black segregated schools had long disproven the arguments segregationists circulated about Blacks being unwilling or unable to learn.

Like the experiences of Reverend Berryman and Clara Johnson, Shirley Nunnally Earley also had relationships with teachers who made an impact on her life. She would describe one of her favorite teachers with fondness: "Marion Anderson . . . was my first-grade teacher. I just thought she was marvelous! She could play the piano and after our work was finished she would play the piano and teach us songs. It was great. We learned. It was a time when your teachers at lunchtime might take us to visit her home. If she needed something from home she would take some of us in her car." Filling the shoes of teachers like Marion Anderson would be difficult for Free School teachers some four years later, but Bernetta Watkins's reflection demonstrates why teachers like James B. Cooley and Willie Mae Watson were integral to the success of the program: they modeled a similar pedagogy of care.

As a child, Watkins was so enthusiastic about school that she begged her mother to let her start when her older sister began first grade. She did attend with her sister for two or three months, until the school checked her birth certificate and declared her too young. For Watkins, this was a great disappointment: "I wasn't happy with that. I was very disappointed. I call it my unofficial kindergarten because, you know, they didn't have kindergarten back then anyway." Her short time attending the first grade with her sister provided her with happy memories of that experience: "Oh, it was fun! I remember the teacher's name, the students, the lessons, the punishments. I remember saying grace before lunch and having devotions, and stuff that they don't do in schools now. I was actually able to read, I learned because for some reason I was spelling and it was intriguing to me to spell backwards as well as forward." Like the others, Watkins's experience was positive in part because of being in an environment where teachers expressed care and concern for their students' learning and happiness. In the context of segregated schooling, where resources were often far below the level of what was found in white schools, the investment of care, concern, and love that was given to black students was often immeasurable.

Stories such as these disprove the arguments offered by proponents of Massive Resistance, which suggested that the Black community didn't care about education. Similarly, they pointed to the refusal of the Black community to accept their help in creating a segregation academy after the public school closures as proof of lack of interest in education. The interviewees' descriptions of their attempts to keep their skills fresh give the lie to these arguments.

Reflections on the Closure Period

The Prince Edward public schools closed without any real notice for Black students and families. The community was left reeling to pick up the pieces. As described in chapter 2, there were a number of attempts to help the Black children continue to have access to learning outside of the home. PECCA's crash courses and parents teaching children in the home were a few of the primary means by which Black students were able to continue their educations. Some parents were able to relocate, either their entire families or just the children, to other counties so that they could continue school. Often, as interview participants revealed, this was the hardest decision parents faced.

Watkins's parents considered sending some of their children to live with their aunts in another county, but since the offer to host did not include all of the children, the parents decided not to break up the family: "My father's thing was, 'I'm not going to break up my family.'" The decision of who would get to leave or who would stay was a personal decision for each family.

Watkins and her siblings were not without access to learning during the closures. While her parents allowed her and her siblings to attend some of the crash programs, her parents had a special arrangement with a local teacher who lived down the road from them. This was a Black first-grade teacher who was without work because of the school closures. Watkins and her siblings attended a night school run by this first-grade teacher, who had taken day work in a neighboring county: "We would walk to her house at night and do work in reading, math, writing, whatever. I don't remember if we did it for all four years, but I know we did it for a time." Efforts such as what Watkins describes and as previously discussed in chapter 2 were dependent on the availability and generosity of those teachers who could offer such services.

For others, continuing their education depended on instruction they could receive at home from their parents. Shirley Earley's mother worked to provide her children with lessons in writing, math, and reading: "My mom helped me learn. We had to read and we practiced cursive writing. My mother worked with us as best she could. For some reason the 4's [multiplication] table was so difficult for me! I don't know why! I remember my mother shedding some tears because some things seemed a bit more difficult for us to get." For many of these parents, taking on the role as educator was not an easy task. Some of the parents did the best they could, but they were themselves victims of unequal educational opportunities and had limited resources and time to dedicate to this new role. Earley's mother was no different, as her own desire to continue her education was met with insurmountable obstacles:

> My mother spent a lot of time with my brother and I. She wasn't an educated person because of how it was in the county and in so many other southern places. It was very difficult for people her age to obtain an education. My mother lived in Baltimore growing up and Dad sent her back to Rice, in Prince Edward, to live with the grandparents to help raise her siblings after her mother passed away. She completed seventh grade in Baltimore, but when they were sent back here the only school they could attend was the school at High Rock that went to seventh grade. She always wanted an education. She went to the seventh grade, again just to be able to go to school, but after seventh grade there was no way for her to get to Farmville to go to high school.

Earley credits those difficult circumstances as being part of why her mother was so committed to helping her children continue their educations. She would go on to say, "When the schools closed here, I get emotional talking about my mother, but when the schools closed here she tried to teach my brother and myself as best she could." The sacrifices made by parents to assist their children did not go unrecognized.

Clara Johnson also attested to the dedication of her mother in helping her to continue her education: "[M]y mom was a proponent of education at home. We did schoolwork at home. . . . That first year just took everyone by surprise, but basically, we did work at home, or we met in other people's houses who taught us and helped us to keep up to par." Like Watkins, Johnson and her siblings would also make use of the close network of community members to supplement their learning. Ultimately, when it appeared that the schools were not going to reopen as quickly as hoped, Johnson and her sisters went to live with a friend of the family in neighboring Cumberland County: "The second year my mom decided to send us to Cumberland schools. My mother had a friend who was the only Black nurse at Southside Hospital, and she lived just over the line. My sister and I would go over and take care of her children while she worked the night shift and we'd go to school with her children in the morning. Then, we'd come back at three and come home and start the cycle all over again." This arrangement was not uncommon, but Cumberland and other counties cracked down on the influx of Prince Edward County students coming through their borders. Many of the counties required that parents pay tuition, making it impossible for some students to attend school there. Eventually Johnson's mother would make the difficult decision to have her children leave Virginia altogether. During the 1962–63 school year, Johnson went to live with an older sister who had married and relocated to Norwalk, Connecticut. The decision for Johnson to leave home was not arrived at easily; her sister helped to convince her mother of the benefit of allowing Johnson and her siblings to move and attend school. For Johnson, being away from her mother and living in a different climate were not easy sacrifices to make: "That was a long ways away and it was cold. My mom and all of us were so close and I missed my mom so much, but I also really wanted to go to school." One of the lessons she took from the experience of going to school in Connecticut was being in a classroom with a white teacher: "We didn't have white teachers here before the schools closed. I knew that you couldn't broad paint the entire white race with one brush; I learned that in Connecticut." Johnson would stay in Connecticut for two years, returning with a bevy of new experiences when the Free Schools opened.

Reverend Berryman's entire family moved in with another family to gain an Appomattox mailing address, allowing the children to attend school there: "We knew people and it was easier to make the transition. The first year we commuted until they found out that we were not residents of Appomattox. Long story short, we eventually had to move into the county to continue to go to school. We kept the home place, in Pamplin, but moved in with another family. We had to have an Appomattox county address." Although this option allowed the family to stay together and the children to continue school, this kind of strategic planning and moving certainly did not come easy and was not an option for many. It certainly caused a disruption for families who had to share resources. For families who did not have the option to move, they were more apt to take advantage of the resources made available in the community.

For Chuckie Reid, his resources for learning after the closures came primarily from the assistance provided in the community. He remembers attending crash courses offered at the local church: "I can't remember exactly what went on, but all I remember is that we didn't go back to school for a while. I ended up going to the church for crash programs, but otherwise, we were young and just thought we didn't have to go to school." Reid, like the others, found his family and church were an immediate source of support and assistance: "In my area, I had my grandma and Reverend Griffin and all of them who helped us when schools were closed. They kept us going through the crash programs and everything. We were still learning. The oldest brothers all went away, and so we were left here, but we were still learning." For each of these participants during the period that access to public education was no longer an option, learning did not cease. No matter the route taken by these families during the closures, their sacrifice and resolve to provide an education for their children was clear throughout these interviews.

Reflections on the Free School Year

The Free School's mission to teach in a way that was connected to helping students navigate and analyze democratic processes suggested a notion that literacy was to be connected to thoughtful democratic participation. As described in the previous chapter, the Free School archive reveals that the primary way this mission was implemented was through crafting a curriculum that encouraged students to bring their interests and experiences into the classroom, providing them opportunities to engage with life outside of Prince Edward and teaching literacy skills in such a way that acknowledged students as capable learners.

Throughout the interviews, it became apparent that most students did not readily recognize the Free School's specific mission of teaching literacy as a means of preparing youth to be active and engaged citizens. What they did remember of the Free School year was, overwhelmingly, the kindness and patience of the teachers and how much the educational efforts that year tried to mimic "normal" schooling. Clara Johnson recognized that her Free School teachers were very dedicated: "The teachers themselves, they were young teachers, some of them in the Free School were barely older than us, but they also cared about what you achieved and it was not that they were just there for the money.... They were here because they wanted to make Farmville a better place and to make us better people.... I felt that, I really did." Her reflection attests to the kind of respect Neil Sullivan encouraged teachers to have for their students, as well as to the pedagogy of care expressed in the curricula designed by Willie Mae Watson and James Cooley. Both respect and care were necessary for students to feel appreciated and comfortable. In particular, Johnson named Ernestine Herndon, a local teacher who stayed in the community and would teach in the Free School, as someone who demonstrated to students that they were important: "She for one always made you feel like you mattered, you do matter in the world and you have something to contribute, and she always expanded on having respect for yourself, respect for other people." Johnson's reflection speaks to the importance of students feeing supported and developing a stronger sense of self-confidence.

Watkins's memories of her year centered on the ordinary. She remembered that most of her day-to-day Free School activities were much like those experienced at the public school when it reopened: "We read aloud. I remember we had worksheets and I remember lots of worksheets and tests. Lots of standardized tests, but other than that I don't remember anything unusual. You wrote on the board, you went to the board and worked problems, you had spelling, and in reading everybody all took turns reading aloud, doing the worksheets after, that's basically what I remember. I don't remember anything that stood out any different from the next year when schools reopened." Watkins's recollections act as evidence that the administrators desired to achieve a fully operating traditional school system. The classroom activities and daily work described and the comparison to schools that reopened the next year all suggest that Watkins felt a sense of normalcy in a program that was created because of a most unique circumstance.

Similarly, Earley described the work teachers did to make learning fun for students: "I remember we used to really enjoy a concentration game the teacher played with us to help students remember concepts. You'd clap your hands and snap your fingers. I just thought they were great." For Earley, in addition to the teachers' enthusiasm she was excited by the opportunity to have extracurricular classes like music: "We had a music teacher and had music on a certain day of the week. It was the first time I'd seen an autoharp and I just thought it was great! Something I'd never seen before, and Mr. Hall, the music teacher, would come down for music and I enjoyed that immensely." These kinds of occasions for play and learning were not taken for granted by students who had gone without access to such opportunities.

While all five interviewees had positive things to say about their Free School experience, there were rightfully some critical observations made about the endeavor. Reverend Berryman recognized the impossibility of building an infrastructure that could meet the needs of such a diverse range of students, but he acknowledged the effort that had to go into the endeavor: "They did, I really believe, the best they could do that first year because there were so many categories and so much was missing. Lots of people complain about this and complain about that, but it was a lot that had to be done to pull everybody back. Just to get everyone back in the academic atmosphere, let alone trying to get it to work after four years, [and] we were still battling with the racial stuff." While the Free School represented the county's first attempt at integration, the "racial stuff" was clearly not going to be remedied within the single year of the Free School's existence.

Other difficulties that were experienced by students were connected to the very things that marked this space as different: the grouping of students in the nongraded curriculum and teachers who were new to the area. Reverend Berryman described the challenges faced by some students in the nongraded grouping:

> They put people in certain grades according to what they were doing and how they measured on the test, but what happened in a lot of the classes, even though you took the test, you still had to take classes where the levels were mixed. The biggest majority of the people that could have been in the class, say you had fifteen in the class, you might have three that was advanced, but you aren't going to have a separate class for three people. In some classes, you were on the same level. Some you just had to go in the class because that was the only class. . . .
>
> Some of the youngsters were like sixteen years old coming to the seventh grade, eighth grade; you know you are four years behind in all that. So, you're growing and having all these human experiences, but yet you are sitting in the same room with somebody younger than you are and most of the time that person younger than you knew more than you did. See, that was demoralizing right from the beginning.

The nongraded grouping may have worked well for those students who were on level, or even advanced, but for those who struggled it was a source of further embarrassment. While the upper unit did utilize tutoring in both math and reading, the sheer magnitude of having such a large group of students at all levels was not easily dealt with due to the limited infrastructure.

Watkins pointed to the problem of having some teachers who did not always understand their students' customs and culture: "In that Free School year we had a lot of teachers from up North who didn't understand southern kids period." The struggle of understanding was probably experienced by student and teacher alike. As I have shown, teachers were consistently reminded of the importance of taking time to listen to students and demonstrate respect, but these are not always easy actions when teachers are still working to understand their students and their communities.

The Free School was designed to provide as close to a normal school experience as possible for students. The interviewees' comments clearly reflect that the results were mixed. The experiences of the students as recorded in the archive and as conveyed to me in interviews with former students demonstrate the complexity of developing a school that could welcome students into its space, acknowledge their unique positions, and allow them some agency in their classrooms. In reflecting on their responses through the interviews, I would argue that none of the former students indicated directly that the Free School was responsible for how they learned what it meant to be a citizen. Nonetheless, rather than view this as the Free School failing to fulfill its mission, we can view these student experiences, as expressed in the interviews, as demonstrating not only the students' awareness and understanding of the Free School as a site that could speak back to racism through education but also their recognition that it would take more than a year of schooling to dismantle the power structure whites had created. Some of the former students I interviewed felt that citizenship training for the Black community in Prince Edward was not solely the responsibility of the schools but of home and church as well.

While schools have typically been recognized as institutions where students are provided access to skills and opportunities that are connected to participating in a democracy, other sites have also provided these kinds of opportunities. For marginalized communities, these alternative spaces, be they churches, social clubs, or home, cannot be overlooked as sites where important lessons about citizenship are learned. Two of the interviewees spoke to this perspective. Reid credited the church and the time Reverend Griffin spent with him as key to both his surviving the closure period and his desire to pursue public office: "It was the church, it was the neighborhood, and being very close to Reverend Griffin's family. He took time with me. We were running *The Voice* newspaper. He kept us doing something." For Reid, the church was a space where he was encouraged to be an active citizen and was provided the support needed to do so. *The Voice* was a church-supported newspaper written by youth and printed in the basement of Reverend Griffin's First Baptist Church. This newspaper prefigured the literacy practices directly connected to citizenship that the Free School would support by giving Prince Edward's Black youth a forum in which to express their concerns and interests.[1] Similar to Reid, Reverend Berryman also cites the kind of critical thinking and democratic engagement that was already being modeled for him and others in the community: "We didn't fit into any type of culture or society that anyone had for us, so we had to be independent and had to be independent thinkers. We had to be wise enough to be able to work with a culture and society that had us as second-class citizens. We were taught that, because we had to create that to survive. All we had were survival skills from grandma and grandpa, the great-aunts and uncles, mommas, and daddies." For Berryman, critical thinking was not something that was isolated from everyday living and survival. Inside a school or a handbook—these would not be the only places for critical thinking. If the path to expanded citizenship was that narrow, then marginalized communities would have insurmountable obstacles. As Berryman indicated, "we were taught in the home, in the church, in the meetings, and all of the people we had rallying us together because the schools were closed."

The reflections from both Berryman and Reid are an important reminder that critical thinking and democratic participation are not lessons to be taught exclusively in schools. While the Free School may have been seen as an affront to notions about race, literacy, and citizenship held by some in Prince Edward, it was not the only means by which students were learning what it meant to be a citizen. For many of these students, those lessons came primarily from the home or the pulpit. While the school wanted to speak back to Massive Resistance through teaching literacy that was connected to preparation for citizenship and critical thinking, not all students necessarily received the school's message this way. The work of speaking back to an unequal system in Prince Edward was done in both public and private spaces in the Black community. From the pulpit to the dinner table, these spaces were able to function without the surveillance of the white community and, as such, were able to be freer with regard to how they approached teaching citizenship and activism. The Free School could not have emulated these types of spaces, not with the stakeholders who were involved. That does not suggest that its mission was for naught, but it points to the complicated endeavor of building institutions and programs that seek to use literacy as a means to prepare students for lives as citizens.

5

Pomp and Circumstance

The Legacy of the Prince Edward County Free School Association for Contemporary Literacy Theory and Pedagogy

THE SENIOR CLASS SONG

God has made us strong; now we belong to thee
He has proved himself so faithfully you see

Though we have been so hurt for four long painful years now we are back
together and we will
Share no more tears

Each and every day as we go our way, faith unlocks
The Door so we can concentrate, John Fitzgerald
Kennedy is only asleep at rest so we must say
For us "God Bless."

PRINCE EDWARD COUNTY FREE SCHOOL ASSOCIATION,

GRADUATING CLASS 1964

On May 25, 1964, the US Supreme Court ruling in the case of *Griffin v. School Board of Prince Edward County* declared Prince Edward's school closings unconstitutional. Almost ten years to the day since the first *Brown* ruling, Justice Hugo Black authored the decision, stating that "there has been entirely too much deliberation and not enough speed in enforcing the constitutional rights which we held in *Brown v. Board of Education*" ("Griffin v. School Board").[1] In the months to follow, Prince Edward County's board of supervisors would barely raise itself to the challenge of reopening schools. Begrudgingly, the board of supervisors approved a bleak spending plan for 1964–65, budgeting only $189,000 to run the public schools, based on the assumption that only sixteen hundred students—roughly the number of children in Prince Edward who were attending the Free School units—would attend the public schools. The board believed that the majority of the county's white students would continue to attend the private, segregated Prince Edward Academy, and by underfunding public schools, the supervisors were setting the stage to fulfill that prophecy. Most of the white families with children enrolled in the Prince Edward Academy kept them there, and the county would continue to disburse funds for the private school through tuition grants.[2] Jill Ogline Titus's description of the tactics used by the county board of supervisors demonstrates their "lawful" defiance of court orders: "Assuming that Black parents would be so grateful to have schools for their children that they would not dare complain about their quality, the supervisors channeled the bulk of county educational funds to the Academy, starved the public schools, and shifted the blame for the chaotic conditions in the reopened buildings onto Black students and parents" (161). This tactic was the same one that had been used since at least the middle of the nineteenth century: take an action that negatively impacts the Black population, but, at the same time, blame the Black community for the action. In the decade that followed, Prince Edward County would have much work to do to help heal the public school system. As with any issue so large, it would take years, with changes in leadership and social customs, to do this work. The county continues to heal.[3]

For the Black community, the reopening of the public schools marked a period of hope as well as recognition that, yet again, the law would do little to change public attitudes about the rights of the Black community with regard to access to equal educational opportunities and resources. Reverend Griffin, knowing that the battle would have to continue, said in a letter to William vanden Heuvel, "We suffered our children to be destroyed so that the law might speak. The law has spoken. We have yet to see it obeyed" (qtd. in Titus 161). Griffin's work in Prince Edward as both a spiritual leader and civil rights activist would continue until his death in 1980. Before the battle for equality in the reopened public schools continued, there was a brief moment for celebration.

The Free School held its graduation on June 15, 1964. Twenty-three students marched down the aisle of the Moton High School in front of family, friends, teachers, and classmates to receive their diplomas. Neil Sullivan reflected: "How many good memories this year had brought to these young people—not just these twenty-three graduates, but all fifteen hundred and seventy-eight of the students enrolled in the Free Schools. And how great had been the accomplishments of these once almost-forgotten children of Prince Edward County; in only ten months' time, they had (by test proof) advanced an average of two years scholastically. Some boys and girls had advanced three and even four years in that time" (*Bound* 211). Sullivan lauded the accomplishments made during the year under the most unique set of circumstances possibly ever seen in the history of public education in the United States. In no other community had a county's board of supervisors deemed it necessary to close public schools as retaliation against *Brown*, and in no other community did more than fifteen hundred children and their parents have to cobble together educational resources under such distressing circumstances. The Free School marked the first time since Reconstruction that the federal government would be involved with the establishment of a school system.

Sullivan, as well as teachers and students, had reason to celebrate the many positive things that happened. There were a number of students in the graduating class who received scholarships to attend college. The class valedictorian, Grace Poindexter, received a scholarship from St. Paul's College in Lawrenceville, Virginia. The salutatorian, John Branch, received a scholarship from Virginia State College, as did the senior class secretary, Betty Ward (Sullivan, *Bound* 209). Recollections from the interviewees in chapter 4 also indicate achievement. All five would go on to be placed in the grade they should have been in if the schools had not been closed. By many measures, the 1964–65 school year was in fact a success. However, there were a number of issues that the Free School's presence did not seem to change.

Given the circumstances, as well as some of the advances made by Free School students, teachers, and administration, Sullivan was right to be proud and congratulatory on the occasion of the Free School graduation. However, it is imperative to examine the Free School's larger mission, specifically, to question whether it met the goal of helping students in their journeys to becoming citizens through its curricula and pedagogies. The Free School, its mission, integrated faculty, and students were an affront to Massive Resistance and the ideologies that placed whites in control of Black lives. An integrated board and teaching staff served an integrated student body. The Free School countered what segregationists said could never or should never happen. This institution served up a response.

At the surface, the Free School's presence did little to change the minds of some whites in Prince Edward. They continued their resistance to integration by underfunding public schools and putting money into the segregated academy. However, even with the Free School's inability to change some of the racist underpinnings of Prince Edward society, what the school was able to accomplish was both pragmatic and bold.

The Free School was a response to Prince Edward's dire situation. The federal government decided to intervene both as a response to the petitions and advocacy and out of fear. First, fears abounded that Prince Edward's stance against integration would spread across the region and possibly the nation. Second, there was growing concern about how the United States would be viewed globally as a leader of democratic nations when it did not treat its own citizens with respect. This does not suggest that the Free School was intended only to help save the country's reputation as the leading democratic superpower, but it does speak to larger issues about what kind of impetus it took for the community to receive aid. Still, there was very real and important work done in these classrooms that had an impact on the students. There were wins in the form of members of the graduating class attending college and other students learning to read after a four-year absence from school. The Free School's focus on literacy was practical and necessary. Reading instruction is typically acknowledged as a core function of school. It was necessary, because the skills gained were needed to help assist and further aid students in thinking critically about democracy (Sullivan, *Bound* 63). Literacy was believed to be a way to prepare students to be engaged citizens. Two questions remain: Would the larger Prince Edward community be responsive to their acquired skills? Would literacy be enough to improve students' lives and sustain commitment to improving conditions in their society?

The effect of literacy programs with regard to citizenship cannot be assessed quantitatively. In part, as scholars have noted, the very definition of what counts as "engaged" or "critical" citizenship behavior stemming from literacy training is in flux. I return to the claims and questions advanced by Amy Wan, who challenges literacy instructors to specifically define what kinds of habits and behaviors are meant to be outcomes of literacy instruction: "How do we know what to do, or if we are even successful?" (17). The Free School's mission statement sought to have students interrogate their democracy through teaching "*more* than just reading, writing, and arithmetic" (Sullivan, "Prince Edward County Free School Association" [Handbook] 3). Did these literacy practices make these students engaged citizens? Asked another way, did the literacy program, the pedagogies practiced by teachers, and the work done by students produce moments of resistance to the discourse of white supremacy put in place by Massive Resistance? How were students prepared for participation as both local and global citizens? I believe that the Free School's legacy offers a complicated response, one that holds implications for literacy instructors today.

Certainly, on one level, teacher-administrators like Willie Mae Watson and James Cooley, or the Free School as a whole, were not going to be able to undo years of systematic discrimination and inequality. They were able to effect change by establishing classroom spaces that helped to welcome students, respect their ways of knowing, and provide them with access to learning that had previously been denied. They made a statement by enacting these pedagogical moves in the face of Massive Resistance. Encouraging teachers to support students, their knowledge and experiences, and expressions of citizenship in the classroom was no easy feat. Students who refused to say the Pledge of Allegiance were exercising their own expressions of citizenship just as much as the students who participated in the voter registration drive or those who wrote poems about the school closures. Teachers made room for and bore witness to the multitude of student expressions and discourses surrounding citizenship. These efforts were as critical as the teaching of phonics for preparing students to be engaged citizens. Black and white teachers offered a demonstration of commitment to students. They were signals that students belonged and that they had a right to bring their knowledge and experiences into the classroom. These moves sound simple but are challenging to put into practice. These practices were necessary for marginalized students who had been told they did not belong and had been cut off from these spaces. But were they enough?

To return to the question posed by Bradford Stull, Is it possible for composition (literacy) to serve in the development of a just society? The Free School does not offer all of the answers to questions like this, but it does provide us with a most intriguing set of possibilities to reflect upon if we are to continue to invest in literacy as a means for developing a just and equitable society. The Free School's curriculum articulated literacy as integral to democratic preparation. This belief was certainly reflected in arguments for *Brown*, but the pedagogies had to deliver the curriculum in such a way that it would be meaningful to students. This history demonstrates the important links between literacy curricula that help prepare students for what it means to be both a local and a global citizen and pedagogies that recognize the worth of students and local communities. While the school wanted to speak back to Massive Resistance through teaching literacy citizenship and critical thinking, students may not necessarily have been conscious of this intent.

The archival documents and interviews with former students tell us that there is more to the story of how these students understood citizenship and how it is taught. Each of the interviewees recounted experiences outside of school in which they witnessed expressions of citizenship. There were parents who fought for school transportation, a father who refused to kowtow to whites, and peers helping to run a community newspaper from the basement of a church. These stories tell us that students come into classrooms with myriad ways of understanding citizenship practices and expressions from within their local communities. Discussions and education about citizenship must account for varied understandings of what the term "citizenship" means. If we are talking about citizenship as the status of a person recognized under law, then discussion of history, civics, and skills that aid people are necessary. However, if we are to also account for cultural citizenship, which the social analysts Stuart Hall and David Held define as citizenship that is also about participation in a "discussion, and a struggle over, the meaning and scope of membership in the community in which one lives" (qtd. in Rosaldo 2–3), then we have to make certain that we allow our literacy programs to be expansive enough to recognize the varied ways in which communities make these expressions and exercise their struggles. The Free School was successful in this regard.

The Free School also reminds us of the power of local resources in reassembling citizenship. Scholars in rhetoric and composition have directed our attention to the importance of the local context for literacy programs that seek to build and acknowledge meaningful relationships between students and their communities (Gold; Ostergaard and Wood). Much of the success the Free School achieved reflected the leadership of locals. Reverend Griffin and Jean Fairfax worked tirelessly to bring Prince Edward's plight to the White House. Once the problem was identified and a plausible solution was in place, it was the leadership of teachers like Watson and Cooley, who knew the community, and their ability to craft pedagogies responsive to their students' needs that made the effort fruitful. What made Watson's and Cooley's pedagogies successful was their recognition that Free School students came with valuable experiences that needed to be recognized and respected. As Kara Miles Turner attests, this kind of recognition was radical: "In Black Belt Virginia of the early 1950s, it could not be taken for granted that Black children would believe themselves entitled to equality with whites. They were surrounded by negative signals about Black abilities, intelligence, and attractiveness. While the county newspaper, the *Farmville Herald*, was packed with accounts of white accomplishments, Black achievements were generally consigned to a brief Colored News Column" (Turner, "Liberating Life-scripts" 90). While Turner focuses on the 1950s in particular, some ten years later not much had changed. Both Watson and Cooley welcomed their students as citizens who continued to grow as people during the school closures. They recognized their innate dignity, no matter Black or white. Practices such as Watson's "talk-time" and Cooley's work-study program recognized the unique needs of a student body that had experienced the school closures and the degrading language of segregationists.

The Free School is a case study for how pedagogies that recognize students' life experiences are integral for learning environments and for supporting efforts to enact citizenship and to speak back to ideologies that support systemic racism. Put simply, if we believe that part of our mission in the teaching of writing is to help citizens to hone skills and practices that will be useful to them as engaged citizens, our classrooms must show students that they matter and their communities matter. This is imperative if we are to help students effect change within those communities. Traditional notions of how we understand literacy often conceive of the curricula as being of service to the individual student. However, these notions still work under the assumption that literacy is a skill or set of skills tied to individuals and their own ability to enact change. The notion that literacy is a vehicle that helps an individual "make it" is troubling. We would be better served by thinking about literacy programs as a service to an entire community. Societal and systemic oppression typically are not undone by single individuals. The individual empowers and mobilizes communities to do the work that needs to be done. We must reconceptualize our classrooms and imagine how a curriculum might be of service to a multitude of communities.

I am calling for us to think about how our classrooms can be better connected to the larger communities in which they reside rather than how our curricula might serve students in their own individual lives. This means developing a stronger recognition that teaching literacy can be a means of helping develop citizenship. There are myriad of ways this may be accomplished through thoughtful connections made with institutions and stakeholders outside of the university. Eli Goldblatt describes the careful work required to cultivate educational experiences that go beyond the college curriculum (2). What I am arguing for is that, in addition to these kinds of relationships, we should also work to center our students' communities in the work of the classroom. Our students may or may not be invested in the local community that surrounds the university. This is not to say that we shouldn't try to cultivate opportunities to get students into those communities through internships or service learning project but to reinforce the importance of better understanding our students, the communities they value, and the types of citizenship they wish to enact. Further, we must understand that there are a variety of literacies and citizenship practices that our students value and practice. They will take these practices with them but will also continue to grow and develop new ones as they travel to new or familiar places. Just as there was no possible way the Free School could walk back four years without schooling, much less more than one hundred years of systemic oppression, there is no one way that a single, insulated writing or literacy curriculum can provide students with everything they need to practice and understand citizenship. To respond to Bradford Stull's question that I raised in the introduction, "Can composition (literacy) serve a just society?" my answer is yes, but not in a way that will be easily replicated for every type of literacy program in various types of institutions.

A responsible and engaged citizenry is the product of multiple factors. Free School students came into the classroom with many ways of knowing and understanding the world. A large number of them, as the interviews and teacher reports attest, had good models of citizenship. Whether it was Reverend Griffin's sermons on Sunday or family wisdom and experiences, these were the epistemologies students brought with them into the classroom. Citizenship training was occurring not only in schools but across a multitude of locations. The real-world teachers of citizenship were as varied as the locations—preachers, housewives, tradesmen, and farmers—each with a range of literacy levels and educations. Our job is to make space for all of these practices to come into the classroom. Tying traditional notions about literacy to citizenship is one way that oppressors exert power and control over who is and who is not a citizen. One way to subvert this pattern of control is to demonstrate to students that there is not just one way to be a citizen and that there are a variety of literacy traditions that can support an engaged citizenry. Teachers can emphasize to students that all of their literacy practices can serve them in their quest to be citizens.

As I have stated, the focus on literacy as a means to prepare students to participate in democratic processes was not new to the Free School. Not only was this a hallmark of education, but it was a fundamental part of the Black community's quest for literacy, extending all the way back to the origins of slavery in America. Stolen from their homes and forced to work under laws and languages that were not their own, slaves recognized English as a symbol of both oppression and liberation—it was both the language of the oppressor and at times the only common tongue available to Africans coming from diverse places. In an end-of-year reflection, one of the Free School elementary principals, Charles Jarrell, boldly proclaimed the aim for the program: "Our aim has been to train children in the understanding and use of their native language" (Jarrell 4). Teachers believed that students in the Free School had a *right* to claim, learn, and use English as their own, no matter the beliefs espoused by those who doubted Blacks' educational abilities. Access to literacy allowed the Black community to speak back to dominant hegemonies, imagine different possibilities, and collaborate for change. The Free School was part of a legacy of institutions whose aim was to deliver literacy instruction for advancement.

In Prince Edward County, the white community's determination to withhold access to literacy as an expression of citizenship was rooted in racialized conceptions of citizenship. Today, it is hard to imagine a community closing its public schools as a means to maintain segregation. However, many of the notions about citizenship and literacy that haunted the pre- and post-*Brown* era persist nonetheless. Definitions of citizenship connected to racist ideologies and polices coupled with continued claims that all people need to do is to pull themselves up by their bootstraps via literacy make us unable to see the lingering systemic ills that plague us.

The Free School provides us with an example of the complicated relationship between literacy and citizenship. Educational institutions have used literacy as a mechanism to both construct the ideal citizen and uphold certain ideologies about citizenship. The proponents of Massive Resistance believed that they were performing their civic duty by withholding education because integration went against their "mores and traditions." The Free School's decision to use a curriculum that closely matched that of other public schools suggests that there was both a hope in literacy and a desire to reclaim it for these students. No, the Free School did not abolish racism in Prince Edward, but its message and actions did not go unnoticed.

The Free School carried out its commitment to literacy in a number of ways. Its curriculum, with its own set of ideologies, challenged the notion that Black children were not worthy of a traditional education and were not capable of traditional literacy skills. The Free School's decision to teach students Standard English and literacy skills was not unique. As scholars in literacy studies, education, and rhetoric and composition have articulated, literacy has been yoked to citizenship, for better or for worse. The type of citizenship the Free School set forth was intended to have students think critically and be able to respond appropriately to "truths and untruths." To enact this citizenship, students needed traditional literacy skills delivered in a way that acknowledged their dignity, community, and values. Thus, we see school documents calling on teachers to listen to their students, making room for students to talk as they liked, and, in the upper unit, bridging the gap between work and school for those students who needed both. Literacy and citizenship in the Free School were inherently tied to the needs of the community served.

Amy Wan argues that "how a nation defines, constructs, and produces citizens communicates not only the ideals of that nation, but also its anxieties, particularly in moments of political, cultural, and economic uncertainty" (1). The type of citizenship being constructed by those whites in power in Prince Edward suggested that control over the Black community through segregation was necessary for society to function. It implied that Blacks need not have an education to find a place in the community. The Free School countered this stance by offering a type of instruction that defined literacy as a means to prepare its students to be citizens who could "sift the truths from the untruths." The Free School's educational response challenged the notion that whites held the truth and were in control over how it was to be understood. Would the Black community of Prince Edward be able to counter the kind of political and cultural disenfranchisement found in their community through literacy?

The simple answer is no. Countering the disenfranchisement of entire groups of people has never successfully been done with only one strategy. One need only look at Prince Edward's history and the history of Blacks in the United States after *Brown* to see that equal access did not solve all of the problems marginalized communities faced then, or now. If we focus on the individual in criticizing the connection between citizenship and literacy, we lose site of the larger system of inequality at work. I believe that while the Free School could not make a dramatic change for its students in a single academic year, the hope and desire for literacy as a possibility for mobility, change, and action remain significant. There is no way to fully measure the school's outcomes. Assessing literacy education and its connection to citizenship is never easy. How does one measure how citizenship is practiced? Do we count votes? Expect that people will participate in town hall meetings or run for local council? Clearly, to be a good citizen it is not necessary to participate in every town hall meeting or to run for office. One learns what it is to be a citizen and exercise citizenship both in what we are taught as well as in what is missing. The interviews from former students demonstrate the importance of learning and seeing citizenship modeled both in school and at home.

As discussed in chapter 1, Danielle Allen writes that *Brown* was a moment where citizenship became unwoven. The period of implementing integration provided opportunities to reconstitute and reimagine citizenship in the United States. We must also reimagine and reconstitute our approach to literacy connected to citizenship. This was a time to rebuild the notion of citizenship, as well as the methods used to obtain skills necessary for participating in a democratic nation. What followed *Brown* I and II is perhaps most revealing of the deep commitment our nation has exhibited toward using race and literacy to control who is recognized as a full citizen and participant in America's democracy. The litany of subsequent court cases that followed *Brown* confirms that, rather than welcome all children into integrated schools, many localities persisted in their commitment to unequal opportunity and access. What then are the lessons and implications about citizenship and literacy that arise from understanding the events that transpired in Prince Edward?

Perhaps, more than pedagogical implications, curricula, or teaching, the legacy of the Free School goes beyond what happened in the classroom. The strength and dedication of the Black community made the Free School happen. The community mobilized during the school closures to continue to provide their children with educational opportunities. They petitioned President Kennedy to respond. Those men and women, farmers, housewives, truck drivers, domestics, preachers, and teachers stood strong against segregated schools, and they mobilized to work for the education of their community. These actions tell us about not only race, literacy, and citizenship but the rhetorics and literacies that are part of the survival strategies for Black lives.

Literacy education and pedagogies that work against racism will never have a one-size-fits-all model, and we would do a disservice to the communities we serve if we try only to replicate previous models. The Free School does, however, provide us with crucial reminders. First, we must acknowledge the epistemologies that exist in the communities we seek to serve. We must listen before we speak, and Krista Ratcliffe's work in the area of rhetorical listening is one possible method for doing so. Her description of rhetorical listening, one that I have also discussed, when, for example, attempting to understand artifacts in the archive, details a means by which we may become aware of our students' home epistemologies. This kind of listening requires an action on the part of the listener. As Ratcliffe says, it "signifies a stance of openness that a person may choose to assume in relation to any person, text, or culture" (17). This stance is not always easy to adopt, especially in the face of students who may bring any number of problematic discourses into the classroom, such as racist or sexist arguments. However, for those literacy instructors who see citizenship preparation as one facet of what they teach, this is part of helping students, and ourselves, learn to have difficult conversations. Part of being a citizen often involves navigating difficult conversations; these can be opportunities to help model behavior or to *witness* to student behavior as they have these kinds of discussions or write about these topics.

Second, this history provides another example of the difficulty involved in using literacy programs to craft responses to white supremacist ideologies and of the importance of recovery efforts that help us to complicate our understanding of the connections between literacy, race, and citizenship. For those instructors and administrators who are committed to using literacy as a method for challenging social inequalities, we need to look to the past to understand how this is a continuum of work. We need more histories that demonstrate the challenges of this work, that show us both the pitfalls and possibilities, so that we might reflect and better understand the ways in which literacy has been successful in this work and has also hindered it.

Many contemporary literacy programs at both the K–12 and postsecondary levels continue to mark literacy as a key component of citizenship. Students are encouraged to think of literacy as a tool that can be wielded for both their own good and the good of others. There is no doubt that literacy has power, but how we engage students, how we respect their communities, how we teach them the skills and the power and ideology behind these skills is the real challenge. No literacy program or initiative comes without its own ideologies, even those that are the most altruistic in trying to provide students with opportunities to use their own voice and communicate their own stories. There are still risks in that work, and for some students, like those who attended the Free School, the stakes can be high. While they must learn the literacies that are most recognized by those in power, we should not ask them to lose the literacies and epistemologies of home. How do we find that balance? This was the challenge Free School teachers faced, and it is a question with which we must continue to reckon. As we continue to recover social histories of literacy that demonstrate the complex connections between literacy, race, and citizenship, perhaps these windows to the past will also act as mirrors by which we can examine and reflect on our own progress.

The Free Schools gave students back one year of schooling out of the five they were denied at the hands of the county's board of supervisors, but they could never fully compensate for all that was lost, nor did the Free School effort necessarily change the behaviors and beliefs of many in the white community who remained steadfast in their belief that Blacks and whites should be segregated. What the Free School represents is part of a greater legacy of the messiness of literacy, race, and citizenship. It is our job to untangle these histories, examine these moments, and unpack the connections in an effort to see how they operate so that further progress can be made in the struggle for human rights.

Appendix

Timeline of Key Local, Regional, and National Events
Related to Civil Rights

The initial point on the timeline is the 1951 student walkout at the segregated Moton High School, and the final point is the opening of integrated public schools in Prince Edward County in 1964. Prepared by H. Robertson.

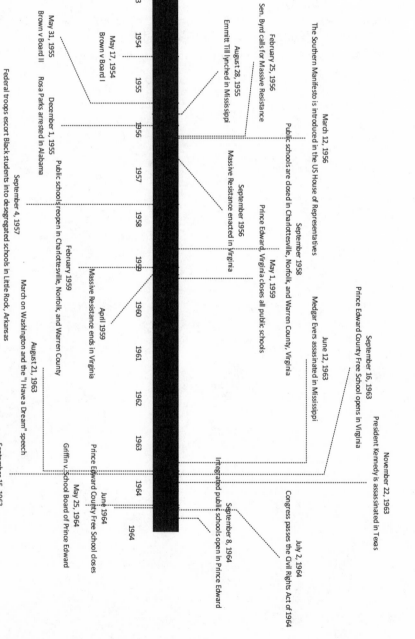

April 23, 1951
Student walkout at Moton High School

1951

1952

1953

1954

1955

1956

1957

1958

1959

1960

1961

1962

1963

1964

1964

May 17, 1954
Brown v Board I

May 31, 1955
Brown v Board II

August 28, 1955
Emmitt Till lynched in Mississippi

December 1, 1955
Rosa Parks arrested in Alabama

February 25, 1956
Sen. Byrd calls for Massive Resistance

March 12, 1956
The Southern Manifesto is introduced in the US House of Representatives

September 1956
Massive Resistance enacted in Virginia

September 4, 1957
Federal troops escort Black students into desegregated schools in Little Rock, Arkansas

September 1958
Public schools are closed in Charlottesville, Norfolk, and Warren County, Virginia

February 1959
Public schools reopen in Charlottesville, Norfolk, and Warren County

April 1959
Massive Resistance ends in Virginia

May 1, 1959
Prince Edward, Virginia closes all public schools

June 12, 1963
Medgar Evers assassinated in Mississippi

August 21, 1963
March on Washington and the "I Have a Dream" speech

September 15, 1963
16th Street Baptist Church bombed in Alabama

September 16, 1963
Prince Edward County Free School opens in Virginia

November 22, 1963
President Kennedy is assassinated in Texas

May 25, 1964
Griffin v. School Board of Prince Edward

June 1964
Prince Edward County Free School closes

July 2, 1964
Congress passes the Civil Rights Act of 1964

September 8, 1964
Integrated public schools open in Prince Edward

Notes

Preface

1. The naming of people of African descent often varies by personal choice. During the 1950s and 1960s, the terms "Negro," "colored," and "Black" were the descriptors most often used. Throughout this manuscript, I alternate between "Black" and "African American," depending on the time period being discussed, reserving "African American" for more contemporary discussions, given that it was not a term widely in circulation during the time period on which this book is focused.

Introduction

1. For more on the Black freedom struggle as it relates to language and literacy, see Geneva Smitherman's *Talkin and Testifyin: The Language of Black America* (1985) and her *Talkin That Talk: Language, Culture, and Education in African America* (1999); Marcyliena Morgan's *Language, Discourse and Power in African American Culture* (2002); and bell hooks's *Teaching to Transgress: Education as the Practice of Freedom*.

Chapter 1. Rhetoric, Race, and Citizenship in the Heart of Virginia

1. The NAACP's legal history recounts that Charles Hamilton Houston took the recommendations from a study by Nathan Margold showing that segregation was never equal. Houston refined Margold's findings and began to argue for equalization. In part, the theory behind arguing for equalization was that many southern locales would not be able to afford to establish separate institutions that were equal to those of whites. Several cases were won from this strategy, including *Murray v. Maryland* (1935), which resulted in the desegregation of the University of Maryland's law school. For more, see Mark V. Tushnet's *The NAACP's Legal Strategy against Segregated Education, 1925–1950* (2005).

2. Prendergast also critiques *Brown* for stalling the civil rights movement. While I do not subscribe to that belief, others have argued that *Brown* had serious shortcomings. See Derrick Bell's *Silent Covenants: "Brown v. Board of Education" and the Unfulfilled Hopes for Racial Reform* for an analysis of *Brown*'s deficiencies with regard to enforcement of true equality.

3. For more on this history, see Melvin Patrick Ely's *Israel on the Appomattox: A Southern Experiment in Black Freedom from the 1790s through the Civil War*.

4. Robert Russa Moton High School was named after Robert Russa Moton, a prominent Black educator and author. Moton was raised in Rice, a small unincorporated community in Prince Edward. He would serve as commandant of cadets at Hampton Institute,

one of the leading historically Black colleges in Virginia, and would go on to serve as principal of Tuskegee Institute after the death of Booker T. Washington. Moton's work would not be bound by employment in academia. He would also serve in a number of public service roles for Pres. Woodrow Wilson and the American National Red Cross. Like his close friend Booker T. Washington, he had conservative views on race relations. He believed that rather than fight for an end to segregation, the Black community should cooperate with whites and focus on advancing themselves through education (Heinemann).

5. Dr. Daniel presented a letter from the college's librarian, Wallace Van Jackson, to the Free School's Board. This letter provided justification for processing and archiving the Free School's papers. Van Jackson's letter included both logistical reasons for the college to maintain the holdings—"Our Special Collections Room is equipped with locked book cases with metal grilled doors. . . . The room will soon be air-conditioned"—and the rationale that the college had a focus on archives that would help researchers interested in "source materials on the Negro." Wallace Van Jackson to President Robert P. Daniel, 14 July 1964, Folder 15, Box 2, Prince Edward County Free School Association Papers 1963–67, Johnston Memorial Library, Virginia State University, Ettrick, Virginia.

6. I credit my knowledge and experience of this term "all our relations" to Malea Powell's use. Powell suggests that the term arose in indigenous communities as a way to describe a particular "philosophy of humans in relation to other living things—plants, animals, rocks, earth—that emphasizes the intricately connected web of relationship that sustains our mutual ability to live out our shared existence on the earth together" ("All Our Relations").

Chapter 2. Manufacturing and Responding to White Supremacist Ideology the Virginia Way

1. There is general consensus among historians that while most scholarship about the South's reaction to *Brown* focuses heavily on segregationists, the voices of moderates merit equal attention. While I agree that a focus on segregationists presents the South as more homogeneous than it was, moderates have less bearing on this particular project. For more on the role of moderates' responses to *Brown*, see James T. Patterson's *Brown v. Board of Education: A Civil Rights Milestone and Its Legacy* (2002) and Matthew D. Lassiter and Andrew B. Lewis's edited volume, *The Moderates' Dilemma: Massive Resistance to School Desegregation in Virginia* (1998).

2. For more on the history of Massive Resistance, especially outside of Virginia, see Clive Webb's *Massive Resistance: Southern Opposition to the Second Reconstruction* (2005).

3. Arguments for states' rights are not exclusive to southern states, nor have they been used only to maintain institutionalized racism. Debates on the balance of power between federal and state governments have persisted since the Constitutional Convention of 1787; however, states' rights became an ideograph associated with maintaining white power structures during the Civil War. For more on the history of states' rights debates, see Forrest McDonald's *States' Rights and the Union: Imperium in Imperio, 1776–1876* (2000).

4. Richard M. Weaver identifies "god terms" as expressions by which "all other terms are ranked as subordinate." Further, these terms hold such a power that they demand sacrifice and action: "this capacity to demand sacrifice is probably the surest indicator of the 'god term,' for when a term is so sacrosanct that the material goods of this life are rendered up to it, then we feel justified in saying that it is in some sense ultimate" (211–12).

5. The Library of Virginia's digital archive, "*Brown v. Board of Education*: Virginia Responds," contains three letters written by white parents from across the commonwealth and sent to the governor and local school boards. These letters came from those communities where schools were closed. While each of the letters was different, one commonality was that parents expressed their desire to reopen schools and that Massive Resistance seemed outdated and detrimental to the community.

6. Robert Pratt (*The Color of Their Skin*) suggests that Almond, rather than having had a true change of heart, was instead fearful of being sentenced to jail time once the Virginia Supreme Court of Appeals determined that closing schools was a violation of the state constitution's requirement that the state maintain a system of free public schools (11).

7. I use the term "Black church" to describe predominantly Black Christian congregations. Historians have argued for the use of this term as a way to describe how these institutions have functioned as a unit. While Black churches have never existed as a monolith, "most Black churches share a very similar religious culture. Similar scriptural analogies, messages, songs, prayers, symbols, rituals, oratorical styles, and themes of equality and freedom" are shared across denominations and congregations (Calhoun-Brown 169).

8. Here I am referring to the ways that Christianity has been used to promote racism. For example, in the context of American slavery, slave masters often used biblical references to argue for the type of control and ownership they exerted over slaves.

9. PECCA carefully defined its existence and creation as not intending to "replace any organization in the County. Rather, its chief objective is to coordinate and strengthen those agencies already in operation. It seeks to render a much needed religious emphasis to its acts of coordination" (4).

10. For more on Peeples's work in the county and his history in civil rights work across the South, see his memoir, *Scalawag: A White Southerner's Journey through Segregation to Human Rights Activism*.

Chapter 3. "Teaching Must Be Our Way of Demonstrating!"

1. This meeting also included representatives from the Virginia Council on Human Relations, a statewide integrated organization formed to foster communication between communities; the Southern Regional Council, known for its research and reports on conditions in the South; and the Potomac Institute.

2. While I was unable to speak with any of the former white students, Sullivan records the threats made against white families whose children attended the Free School year. The Tew family would relay to Sullivan that Mrs. Tew was threatened in a store. A man told

her, "Your head will be cut off if you let Letitia go to school with the niggers on Monday" (qtd. in Sullivan, *Bound* 82).

3. Harriet A. Woods's 1937 thesis, "A Study of the Origin and Development of the Educational Excursion," traced the development of field trips as a teaching procedure. Woods finds arguments for field trips in materials about curriculum and elementary project-based teaching as early as the 1920s. She argues for educational excursions to be part of the "new conception of education," which focused on the development of the whole child to best provide students with "experiences that will contribute to his desirable growth, mentally, socially, and physically" (9, 10).

Chapter 4. Free School Students Speak

1. The Longwood University archive in Farmville, Virginia, holds digitized copies of *The Voice*. While the newspaper is said to have run from 1962 until sometime around 1967, Longwood's archive has issues from only 1966 and 1967. The newspaper editions from this time period covered a range of topics but were primarily focused on advocating for better resources in the newly opened public schools and covering local and state politics.

Chapter 5. Pomp and Circumstance

1. The two dissenting votes on the decision came from Justices John Marshall Harlan II and Tom C. Clark. Both disagreed that the federal court had the power to order the reopening of public schools but otherwise agreed with the high court's opinion.

2. An editorial in the *Farmville Herald* from Friday, June 26, 1964, cites the court order for the schools to reopen and states that the $189,000 budget, based on an estimated sixteen hundred pupils, demonstrated that "without question, the Prince Edward board of supervisors has obeyed the edict of the federal court in good faith" ("Prince Edward's Good Faith").

3. For a thorough overview of the challenge the county faced after the schools reopened, see Jill Ogline Titus's *Brown's Battleground*.

Works Cited

Adams Karen, and Angela Rainey. "Race, Civil Rights, and Farmville's Multicultural Past." *Two Hundred Years in the Heart of Virginia*, edited by Robert F. Pace, Longwood College Foundation, 1998, pp. 45–60.

Allen, Danielle S. *Talking to Strangers: Anxieties of Citizenship since Brown v. Board of Education*. U of Chicago P, 2006.

Allington, Richard L., and Anne McGill-Franzen. "Looking Back, Looking Forward: A Conversation about Teaching Reading in the 21st Century." *Reading Research Quarterly*, vol. 35, no. 1, 2000, pp. 136–53.

Althusser, Louis. *On the Reproduction of Capitalism: Ideology and Ideological State Apparatuses*. Translated by G. M. Goshgarian, Verso, 2014.

"Around Robin Hood's Barn." Editorial. *Farmville Herald*, 26 July 1963.

Bacon, Jacqueline. *The Humblest May Stand Forth: Rhetoric, Empowerment, and Abolition*. U of South Carolina P, 2002.

Bacon, Jacqueline, and Glen McClish. "Reinventing the Master's Tools: Nineteenth-Century African American Literary Societies of Philadelphia and Rhetorical Education." *Rhetoric Society Quarterly*, vol. 30, no. 4, 2000, pp. 19–47.

Baker, Lee D. *From Savage to Negro: Anthropology and the Construction of Race, 1896–1954*. U of California P, 1998.

Bartley, Numan V. *The Rise of Massive Resistance: Race and Politics in the South during the 1950's*. Louisiana State UP, 1999.

Bell, Derrick. *Silent Covenants: Brown v. Board of Education and the Unfulfilled Hopes for Racial Reform*. Oxford UP, 1990.

Berryman, Rev. Everett. Interview by author, 13 Aug. 2012.

Bland, Lemuel. "End of Year Report." June 1964. Folder 51, Box 49, Prince Edward County Virginia Free School Association, Special Collections and Archives, Virginia State University, Ettrick.

Blythe, Stuart. "Agencies, Ecologies, and the Mundane Artifacts in Our Midst." *Labor, Writing Technologies, and the Shaping of Composition in the Academy*, edited by Pamela Takayoshi and Patricia Sullivan, Hampton Press, 2007, pp. 167–86.

Bonastia, Christopher. *Southern Stalemate: Five Years without Public Education in Prince Edward County, Virginia*. U of Chicago P, 2012.

Bowman, John G. "Letter to Gov. Almond." 4 Apr. 1959. *Brown v. Board of Education*: Virginia Responds, www.lva.virginia.gov/exhibits/brown/bowman.htm. Accessed 25 June 2017.

Brown v. Board of Education of Topeka [I]. 347 US 483 (1954).

Brown v. Board of Education of Topeka [II]. 349 US 294 (1955).

Brundage, W. Fitzhugh. *The Southern Past: A Clash of Race and Memory*. Belknap Press of Harvard UP, 2005.

Brundage, W. Fitzhugh, editor. *Where These Memories Grow: History, Memory, and Southern Identity*. U of North Carolina P, 2000.

Burke, Kenneth. *A Rhetoric of Motives*. U of California P, 1969.

Byrd, Harry, F. *Brown* Press Release. 17 May 1956. Series IV.F, Harry Flood Byrd Papers, 1911–65, Accession #97000, Special Collections, University of Virginia Library, Charlottesville.

Byrd, Harry, F. Letter to the Commission on Education. 1958. Series IV.F, Harry Flood Byrd Papers, 1911–65, Accession #97000, Special Collections, University of Virginia Library, Charlottesville.

Byrd, Harry, F. Untitled document. Undated (but written after May 1959). Series IV.F, Harry Flood Byrd Papers, 1911–65, Accession #97000, Special Collections, University of Virginia Library, Charlottesville.

Calhoun-Brown, Allison. "Upon This Rock: The Black Church, Nonviolence, and the Civil Rights Movement." *PS: Political Science and Politics*, vol. 33, no. 2, 2000, pp. 168–74.

Cardinal Principles of Secondary Education: A Report of the Commission on the Reorganization of Secondary Education, Appointed by the National Education Association. Washington, DC: Government Printing Office.

Childers, Jay P. *The Evolving Citizen: American Youth and the Changing Norms of Democratic Engagement*. Penn State UP, 2013.

"Classes for 'Free' School Set Sept. 16." *Farmville Herald* (Farmville, VA), 20 Aug. 1963, p. 1.

Cobb, James C. *Away Down South: A History of Southern Identity*. Oxford UP, 2005.

Cone, James H. "Black Theology and the Black Church: Where Do We Go from Here?" *CrossCurrents*, vol. 27, no. 2, 1977, pp. 147–56.

Cone, James H. *God of the Oppressed*. Orbis Books, 1997.

Connors, Robert. "Dreams and Play: Historical Method and Methodology." *Methods and Methodology in Composition Research*, edited by Gesa Kirsch and Patricia Sullivan, Southern Illinois UP, 1992, pp. 15–36.

Cooley, James. "Moton Philosophy." N.d. Folder 2, Box 33, Prince Edward County Virginia Free School Association. Special Collections and Archives, Virginia State University, Ettrick.

Cooley, James. "Preliminary Annual High School Report for Robert R. Moton High School, Farmville, VA." N.d. Folder 7, Box 33, Prince Edward County Virginia Free School Association, Special Collections and Archives, Virginia State University, Ettrick.

Cooley, James. "Prince Edward Free School Association: R. R. Moton High School Handbook for Teachers." September 1963. Folder 17, Box 30, Prince Edward County Virginia Free School Association, Special Collections and Archives, Virginia State University, Ettrick.

Cooley, James. "Requirements for Graduation." N.d. Folder 6, Box 31, Prince Edward County Virginia Free School Association, Special Collections and Archives, Virginia State University, Ettrick.

Crawford, Vicki L., Jacqueline Anne Rouse, and Barbara Woods, editors. *Women in the Civil Rights Movement: Trailblazers and Torchbearers, 1941–1965.* Indiana UP, 1990.

Davis, Jefferson. *Jefferson Davis, Constitutionalist: His Letters, Papers, and Speeches.* Edited by Dunbar Rowland, vol. 3, Literary Licensing, 2011.

"The Decision." *Richmond News Leader,* 17 May 1954.

Defenders of State Sovereignty and Individual Liberties. "A Plan for Virginia." Richmond, Virginia, 8 June 1955, Library of Virginia Archives, Richmond.

Defenders of State Sovereignty and Individual Liberties. *Principles for Which We Stand.* Richmond, Virginia, 1955, Library of Virginia Archives, Richmond.

Dohme, Ainslee, and Alvin Dohme. "Letter to County Supervisors." 26 Feb. 1959. *Brown v. Board of Education*: Virginia Responds, www.lva.virginia.gov/exhibits/brown/dohme .htm. Accessed 25 June 2017.

Du Bois, W. E. B. "The Negroes of Farmville, Virginia: A Social Study." *Bulletin of the Department of Labor,* vol. 14, Jan. 1998, pp. 1–38, web.archive.org/web/20080708225716/ http://etext.lib.virginia.edu/toc/modeng/public/DubFarm.html.

Earley, Shirley. Interview by author, 21 Sept. 2015.

Educational Policies Commission. *Education for All American Youth: A Further Look.* Rev. ed. Washington, DC, 1952.

Ely, Melvin Patrick. *Israel on the Appomattox: A Southern Experiment in Black Freedom from the 1790s through the Civil War.* Vintage, 2005.

Enoch, Jessica. *Refiguring Rhetorical Education: Women Teaching African American, Native American, and Chicano/a Students, 1865–1911.* Southern Illinois UP, 2008.

Enoch, Jessica. "A Woman's Place Is in the School: Rhetorics of Gendered Space in Nineteenth-Century America." *College English,* vol. 70, no. 3, 2008, pp. 275–95, www .jstor.org/stable/25472267.

Fairclough, Adam. *A Class of Their Own: Black Teachers in the Segregated South.* Belknap Press of Harvard UP, 2007.

Fairfax, Jean. Letter to Prince Edward County Free School Association Board of Trustees. N.d. Folder 1, Box 1, Prince Edward County Virginia Free School Association, Special Collections and Archives, Virginia State University, Ettrick.

"First Group of Students Arrive." *Farmville Herald* (Farmville, VA), 17 Sept. 1963, p. 1.

"Field Trips." N.d. Folders 3–4, Box 32, Prince Edward County Virginia Free School Association, Special Collections and Archives, Virginia State University, Ettrick.

Fitch, Eliza. "Letter to Gov. Stanley." 26 June 1955. *Brown v. Board of Education*: Virginia Responds, www.lva.virginia.gov/exhibits/brown/fitch.htm. Accessed 25 June 2017.

Foster, Michele. *Black Teachers on Teaching*. New Press Education Series, 1998.

Flesch, Rudolf. *Why Johnny Can't Read: And What You Can Do About It*. Harper & Brothers, 1955.

Gaillet, Lynée Lewis. "Archival Survival: Navigating Historical Research." *Working in the Archives: Practical Research Methods for Rhetoric and Composition*, edited by Alexis E. Ramsey, Wendy B. Sharer, Barbara L'Eplattenier, and Lisa Mastrangelo, Southern Illinois UP, 2010, pp. 28–39.

Gates, Robbins L. *The Making of Massive Resistance: Virginia's Politics of Public School Desegregation, 1954–1956*. U of North Carolina P, 1964.

Gilyard, Keith. "Introduction: Aspects of African American Rhetorics as a Field." *African American Rhetoric(s): Interdisciplinary Perspectives*, edited by Elaine Richardson and Ronald L. Jackson II, Southern Illinois UP, 2007, pp. 1–19.

Gold, David. *Rhetoric at the Margins: Revising the History of Writing Instruction, 1873–1947*. Southern Illinois UP, 2008.

Goldblatt, Eli. *Because We Live Here: Sponsoring Literacy beyond the College Curriculum*. Hampton Press, 2007.

Goodlad, John I., and Robert H. Anderson. *The Nongraded Elementary School*. Teachers College Press, 1987.

Graff, Harvey J. "The Literacy Myth at Thirty." *Journal of Social History*, vol. 43, no. 10, 2010, pp. 635–61.

Graff, Harvey J. *The Literacy Myth: Literacy and Social Structure in the Nineteenth-Century City*. Academic Press, 1979.

Green, Robert L. *The Educational Status of Children in a District without Public Schools*. Michigan State University Bureau of Educational Research, 1964.

Griffin v. School Board of Prince Edward County. 377 US 218 (1964).

Hale, Grace Elizabeth. *Making Whiteness: The Culture of Segregation in the South, 1890–1940*. Vintage Books, 1999.

Harrison, Kimberly. *The Rhetoric of Rebel Women: Civil War Diaries and Confederate Persuasion*. Southern Illinois UP, 2013.

Heinemann, Ronald L. *Harry Byrd of Virginia*. UP of Virginia, 1996.

Hicks, Terence, and Abul Pitre, eds. *The Educational Lockout of African Americans in Prince Edward County, Virginia (1959–1964)*. U of America P, 2010.

hooks, bell. *Teaching to Transgress: Education as the Practice of Freedom*. Routledge, 1994.

Hopkins, Dwight. *Introducing Black Theology of Liberation*. Orbis Books, 1999.

Hurston, Zora Neal. *Folklore, Memoirs and Other Writing*. 2nd ed., Library of America, 1995.

"Is Moton the Best by Your Actions?" Editorial. *Moton Eagle*, 26 Mar. 1964, Box 107, Prince Edward County Virginia Free School Association, Special Collections and Archives, Virginia State University, Ettrick.

Jarrell, Charles. "Report from Free School #3." Monthly Reports, June 1964. Folder 46,

Box 18, Prince Edward County Virginia Free School Association, Special Collections and Archives, Virginia State University, Ettrick.

Johnson, Clara. Interview by author, 11 Aug. 2012.

Jones, Duane. "Letter of Application." August 1963. Folder 15, Box 26, Prince Edward County Virginia Free School Association, Special Collections and Archives, Virginia State University, Ettrick.

Kates, Susan. *Activist Rhetorics and American Higher Education, 1885–1937*. Southern Illinois UP, 2001.

Kates, Susan. "Politics, Identity, and the Language of Appalachia." *Rhetorical Education in America*, edited by Cheryl Glenn, Margaret Lyday, and Wendy Sharer, U of Alabama P, 2004.

Key, V. O. *Southern Politics in State and Nation*. 1949. U of Tennessee P, 1984.

King, Lisa, Rose Gubele, and Joyce Rain Anderson, eds. *Survivance, Sovereignty, and Story: Teaching American Indian Rhetorics*. Utah State UP, 2015.

Kluger, Richard. *Simple Justice: The History of Brown v. Board of Education and Black America's Struggle for Equality*. Vintage Books, 2004.

Kvale, Steinar, and Svend Brinkmann. *InterViews: Learning the Craft of Qualitative Research Interviewing*. 2nd ed., SAGE Publications, 2008.

Kynard, Carmen. *Vernacular Insurrections: Race, Black Protest, and the New Century in Composition-Literacies Studies*. State U of New York P, 2014.

Lassiter, Matthew D., and Andrew B. Lewis. Introduction. *The Moderates' Dilemma: Massive Resistance to School Desegregation in Virginia*, edited by Matthew Lassiter and Andrew B. Lewis, UP of Virginia, 1998, pp. 1–21.

Lee, Brian. "We Will Move: The Kennedy Administration and Restoring Public Education to Prince Edward County, Virginia." *The Educational Lockout of African Americans in Prince Edward County, Virginia (1959–1964)*, edited by Terence Hicks and Abul Pitre, UP of America, 2010, pp. 19–32.

Lee, Brian, and Brian J. Daugherity. "Program of Action: The Rev. L. Francis Griffin and the Struggle for Racial Equality in Farmville, 1963." *Virginia Magazine of History and Biography*, vol. 121, no. 3, 2013, pp. 250–87.

Lipsitz, George. *The Possessive Investment in Whiteness: How White People Profit from Identity Politics*. Temple UP, 2006.

Logan, Shirley Wilson. *Liberating Language: Sites of Rhetorical Education in Nineteenth-Century Black America*. Southern Illinois UP, 2008.

McDonald, Forrest. *States' Rights and the Union: Imperium in Imperio, 1776–1876*. UP of Kansas, 2000.

McGee, Michael. "The 'Ideograph': A Link between Rhetoric and Ideology." *Quarterly Journal of Speech*, vol. 66, no. 1, 1980, pp. 1–16.

McGee, Michael. "In Search of 'the People': A Rhetorical Alternative." *Quarterly Journal of Speech*, vol. 61, no. 3, 1975, pp. 235–49.

"Minutes of First Meeting of the Board of Trustees of the Prince Edward Free School Association." 17 Aug. 1963. Folder 1, Box 1, Prince Edward County Virginia Free School Association, Special Collections and Archives, Virginia State University, Ettrick.

"Minutes of the Third Meeting of the Board of Trustees of the Prince Edward Free School Association." 27 Aug. 1963. Folder 4, Box 1, Prince Edward County Virginia Free School Association, Special Collections and Archives, Virginia State University, Ettrick.

Morgan, Marcyliena. *Language, Discourse and Power in African American Culture*. Cambridge UP, 2002.

Moss, Beverly J. *A Community Text Arises: A Literate Text and a Literacy Tradition in African-American Churches*. Hampton Press, 2003.

Moss, C. G. Gordon. Letter to Colgate W. Darden. 19 Aug. 1963. Folder 2, Box 4, Prince Edward County Virginia Free School Association, Special Collections and Archives, Virginia State University, Ettrick.

Mountford, Roxanne. "On Gender and Rhetorical Space." *Rhetoric Society Quarterly*, vol. 31, no. 1, 2001, pp. 41–71.

Murphy, James J., James Berlin, Robert J. Connors, Sharon Crowley, Richard Leo Enos, Victor J. Vitanza, Susan C. Jarratt, Nan Johnson, and Jan Swearingen. "The Politics of Historiography" [Octalog: 1988 CCCC panel]. *Rhetoric Review*, vol. 7, no. 1, 1988, pp. 5–49.

Murrell, Amy. "The 'Impossible' Prince Edward Case: The Endurance of Resistance in a Southside County, 1959–1964." *The Moderates' Dilemma: Massive Resistance to School Desegregation in Virginia*, edited by Matthew Lassiter and Andrew B. Lewis, UP of Virginia, 1998, pp. 134–67.

Newman, Mark. *Getting Right with God: Southern Baptists and Desegregation*. U of Alabama P, 2012.

"Opening Closed Doors." *Narrative of the American Friends Service Committee's Work in Prince Edward County, Virginia, 1959–1965*, AFSC (American Friends Service Committee), 2004.

"Opening Day Ceremonies." *Richmond Afro-American*, 16 Sept. 1963.

Ostergaard, Lori, and Henrietta Rix Wood, editors. *In the Archives of Composition: Writing and Rhetoric in High Schools and Normal Schools*. U of Pittsburgh P, 2015.

Pahowka, Gareth D. "Voices of Moderation: Southern Whites Respond to Brown v. Board of Education." *Gettysburgh Historical Journal*, vol. 5, article 6, 2006, pp. 44–66. cupola. gettysburg.edu/ghj/vol5/iss1/6.

Patterson, James T. *Brown vs. Board of Education: A Civil Rights Milestone and Its Troubled Legacy*. Oxford UP, 2002.

Pearson, P. David. "American Reading Instruction since 1967." *American Reading Instruction (Special Edition)*, edited by Nila Banton Smith, International Reading Association, 2002, pp. 419–86.

PECCA (Prince Edward County Christian Association). "Operation 1700: A Special Report." N.d. Folder 1, Box 23, Prince Edward County Virginia Free School Association, Special Collections and Archives, Virginia State University, Ettrick.

Peeples, Edward. *Scalawag: A White Southerner's Journey through Segregation to Human Rights Activism*. U of Virginia P, 2014.

"Plan to Ask Cram Course for Va. Pupils Denied School 4 Years." *Chicago Defender*, 13 Apr. 1963, national ed. Accessed at ProQuest, 27 Apr. 2011.

Pough, Gwendolyn. *Check It While I Wreck It: Black Womanhood, Hip-Hop Culture, and the Public Sphere*. Northeastern UP, 2004.

Powell, Malea. "All Our Relations: Contested Space, Contested Knowledge." CCCC: Conference on College Composition Call for Program Proposals, NCTE, 2010, www.ncte.org/library/nctefiles/groups/cccc/convention/2011/4c_callfor_2011b.pdf.

Pratt, Robert A. *The Color of Their Skin: Education and Race in Richmond, Virginia, 1954–1989*. UP of Virginia, 1992.

Prendergast, Catherine. *Literacy and Racial Justice: The Politics of Learning after Brown v. Board of Education*. Southern Illinois UP, 2003.

"Prince Edward Free Schools." *Farmville Herald* (Farmville, VA), 20 Aug. 1963, p. 4A.

"Prince Edward's Good Faith." *Farmville Herald* (Farmville, VA), 26 June 1964, p. 4A.

Raboteau, Albert J. *Slave Religion: The "Invisible Institution" in the Antebellum South*. Oxford UP, 2004.

Ratcliffe, Krista. *Rhetorical Listening: Identification, Gender, Whiteness*. Southern Illinois UP, 2006.

Ravitch, Diane. "Education and Democracy." *Making Good Citizens: Education and Civil Society*, edited by Diane Ravitch and Joseph P. Viteritti, Yale UP, 2003.

Reese, William J. *America's Public Schools: From the Common School to "No Child Left Behind."* Johns Hopkins UP, 2011.

Reid, Armstead D. "Chuckie." Interview by author, 9 Sept. 2015.

Richardson, Elaine. "African American Literacies." *Encyclopedia of Language and Education*, edited by Nancy Hornberger, Springer, 2008, pp. 335–46.

Richardson, Elaine B., and Ronald L. Jackson II, editors. *African American Rhetoric(s): Interdisciplinary Perspectives*. Southern Illinois UP, 2007.

Richardson, Elaine B., and Ronald L. Jackson II, editors. *Understanding African American Rhetoric: Contemporary Origins to Contemporary Innovations*. Routledge, 2003.

Roberts-Miller, Patricia. *Fanatical Schemes: Proslavery Rhetoric and the Tragedy of Consensus*. U of Alabama P, 2010.

Rosaldo, Renato, editor. *Cultural Citizenship in Island Southeast Asia: Nation and Belonging in the Hinterlands*. U of California P, 2003.

Royster, Jacqueline Jones. Foreword. *African American Rhetoric(s): Interdisciplinary Perspectives*, edited by Elaine B. Richardson and Ronald L. Jackson II, Southern Illinois UP, 2004, pp. xi–xii.

Royster, Jacqueline Jones. *Traces of a Stream: Literacy and Social Change among African American Women.* U of Pittsburgh P, 2000.

Rubin, Anne Sara. "Seventy-six and Sixty-one: Confederates Remember the American Revolution." *Where These Memories Grow: History, Memory, and Southern Identity,* edited by W. Fitzhugh Brundage, Belknap Press of Harvard UP, 2005, pp. 85–106.

Schneider, Stephen. *You Can't Padlock an Idea: Rhetorical Education at the Highlander Folk School, 1932–1961.* U of South Carolina P, 2014.

"School Fund Slash Denounced by Prince Edward Clergymen." *Richmond Afro-American,* 27 June 1959, p. 20.

Smith, Bob. *They Closed Their Schools: Prince Edward County, Virginia, 1951–1964.* Farmville, VA: Martha E. Forrester Council of Women, 1996.

Smitherman, Geneva. *The Language of Black America.* Routledge, 1999.

Smitherman, Geneva. *Talkin and Testifyin: The Language of Black America.* Wayne State UP, 1986.

Smitherman, Geneva. *Talkin That Talk: Language, Culture, and Education in African America.* Routledge, 2006.

"Southern Manifesto." *Congressional Record,* 84th Cong., 2nd sess., vol. 102, part 4, 12 Mar. 1956, en.wikisource.org/wiki/Southern_Manifesto. Accessed 10 July 2012.

"Student Evaluation Reports." October 1963. Folders 1–3, Box 29, Prince Edward County Virginia Free School Association, Special Collections and Archives, Virginia State University, Ettrick.

"Student Evaluation Reports." November 1963. Folders 4–9, Box 29, Prince Edward County Virginia Free School Association. Special Collections and Archives, Virginia State University, Ettrick.

Stull, Bradford. *Amid the Fall, Dreaming of Eden: Du Bois, King, Malcolm X, and Emancipatory Composition.* Southern Illinois UP, 1999.

Sullivan, Neil. *Bound for Freedom: An Educator's Adventures in Prince Edward County, Virginia.* Little, Brown, 1965.

Sullivan, Neil. "Bulletin #9." Prince Edward County Free School, September 1963, Folder 3, Box 19, Prince Edward County Virginia Free School Association, Special Collections and Archives, Virginia State University, Ettrick.

Sullivan, Neil. "Bulletin #10." Prince Edward County Free School, September 1963, Folder 3, Box 19, Prince Edward County Virginia Free School Association, Special Collections and Archives, Virginia State University, Ettrick.

Sullivan, Neil. "Bulletin #20." Prince Edward County Free School, September 1963, Folder 3, Box 19, Prince Edward County Virginia Free School Association, Special Collections and Archives, Virginia State University, Ettrick.

Sullivan, Neil. "November Progress Report." November 1963. Folder 1, Box 33A, Prince Edward County Free School Association, Special Collections and Archives, Virginia State University, Ettrick.

Sullivan, Neil. "Prince Edward County Free School Association [Handbook]." August 1963. Folder 23, Box 33, Prince Edward County Virginia Free School Association, Special Collections and Archives, Virginia State University, Ettrick.

"Teacher Roster." N.d. Folder 2, Box 32, Prince Edward County Virginia Free School Association. Special Collections and Archives, Virginia State University, Ettrick.

Tillerson-Brown, Amy. "Grassroots Schools and Training Centers in the Prospect District of Prince Edward County Virginia, 1959–1964." *The Educational Lockout of African Americans in Prince Edward County, Virginia (1959–1964)*, edited by Terence Hicks and Abul Pitre, UP of America, 2010, pp. 1–17.

Tirabassi, Katherine. "Journeying into the Archives: Exploring the Pragmatics of Archival Research." *Working in the Archives: Practical Research Methods from Rhetoric and Composition*, edited by Alexis E. Ramsey, Wendy B. Sharer, Barbara L'Eplattenier, and Lisa Mastrangelo, Southern Illinois UP, 2010, pp. 169–80.

Titus, Jill Ogline. *Brown's Battleground: Students, Segregationists, and the Struggle for Justice in Prince Edward County, Virginia*. U of North Carolina P, 2014.

Turner, Kara Miles. "'Getting It Straight': Southern Black School Patrons and the Struggle for Equal Education in the Pre- and Post-Civil Rights Eras." *Journal of Negro Education*, vol. 72, no. 2, 2003, pp. 217–29.

Turner, Kara Miles. "'Liberating Lifescripts': Prince Edward County, Virginia, and the Roots of *Brown v. Board of Education*." *From the Grassroots to the Supreme Court: Brown v. Board of Education and American Democracy*, edited by Peter F. Lau, Duke UP, 2004, pp. 88–104.

Tushnet, Mark V. *The NAACP's Legal Strategy against Segregated Education, 1925–1950*. U of North Carolina P, 2005.

"1,200 Attend Funeral of the 'Fighting Preacher.'" *The Afro-American* (Baltimore, MD), 2 Feb. 1980.

"Unwarranted Attack." Editorial. *Farmville Herald* (Farmville, VA), 6 Aug. 1963.

US Census. "Census of the Population—1950." Washington, DC: Government Printing Office, 1955.

US Census. "Census of the Population—1960." Washington, DC: Government Printing Office, 1966.

Walker, Vanessa Siddle. *Their Highest Potential: An African American School Community in the Segregated South*. U of North Carolina P, 1996.

Wan, Amy. *Producing Good Citizens: Literacy Training in Anxious Times*. U of Pittsburgh P, 2014.

Watkins, Bernetta. Interview by author, 13 Aug. 2012.

Watson, Willie Mae. "About Prince Edward." N.d. Folder 22, Box 33A, Prince Edward County Virginia Free School Association, Special Collections and Archives, Virginia State University, Ettrick.

Watson, Willie Mae. "Curriculum Notes #5." N.d. Folder 11, Box 34, Prince Edward County Virginia Free School Association, Special Collections and Archives, Virginia State University, Ettrick.

Watson, Willie Mae. "Curriculum Notes #11." N.d. Folder 11, Box 34, Prince Edward County Virginia Free School Association, Special Collections and Archives, Virginia State University, Ettrick.

Watson, Willie Mae. "Guidelines to Curriculum Development for Primary School and Middle School." N.d. Folder 1, Box 34, Prince Edward County Virginia Free School Association, Special Collections and Archives, Virginia State University, Ettrick.

Watson, Willie Mae. "Language for Self-Expression, Communication, Enjoyment, Development, Enrichment." N.d. Folder 12, Box 34, Prince Edward County Virginia Free School Association, Special Collections and Archives, Virginia State University, Ettrick.

Watson, Willie Mae. "Memo to Elementary Principals and Teachers." 4 Apr. 1964. Folder 1, Box 34, Prince Edward County Virginia Free School Association, Special Collectiosn and Archives, Virginia State University, Etrick.

Weaver, Richard M. *The Ethics of Rhetoric.* 1953. Gateway Editions, 1977.

Webb, Clive. *Massive Resistance: Southern Opposition to the Second Reconstruction.* Oxford UP, 2005.

Wells, Rufus. "Inside Prince Edward County, Virginia: What Happens When Schools Are Killed." *Richmond Afro-News Leader,* 26 Sept. 1959, pp. 1–2.

Wells, Rufus. "Prince Edward Residents Seek Solution to School Problems." *Richmond Afro-News Leader,* 15 Aug. 1959, pp. 20–21.

"What about Schools in 64–65?" Editorial. *Moton Eagle,* 17 Feb. 1964, Box 107, Prince Edward County Virginia Free School Association, Special Collections and Archives, Virginia State University, Ettrick.

Whittaker, Katherine. "Letter of Application." August 1963. Folder 15, Box 26, Prince Edward County Virginia Free School Association, Special Collections and Archives, Virginia State University, Ettrick.

Williams, Heather Andrea. *Self-Taught: African American Education in Slavery and Freedom.* U of North Carolina P, 2009.

Wilmore, Gayraud S. *Black Religion and Black Radicalism: An Interpretation of the Religious History of Afro-American People.* 2nd ed. Orbis Books, 1997.

Woods, Harriet A. "A Study of the Origin and Development of the Educational Excursion." MA thesis, State U of Iowa, 1937. ir.uiowa.edu/etd/4940.

Woodward, C. Vann. *The Burden of Southern History.* 3rd ed. Louisiana State UP, 2008.

Van Jackson, Wallace. Letter to President Robert P. Daniel. 14 July 1964. Folder 15, Box 2, Prince Edward County Free School Association Papers, 1963–67, Johnston Memorial Library, Virginia State University, Petersburg.

Index

segregationists: rhetoric of, 29–30, 32–37, 38–40; scholarly focus on, 132n1

sit-ins and protests, 14–15, 53–56, *54, 55,* 61–62

southern identity, 26–29

Southern Manifesto, 32–33

Stanley, Thomas, 31, 34

states' rights, 32–38, 132n3

student council, 90–91

student newspapers, 91–92, 106, 115, 134n1 (chap. 4)

Student Nonviolent Coordinating Committee (SNCC), 17

students: concerns of, 96–103; experiences at Free School, 112–16; experiences at segregated schools, 107–9; experiences during school closures, 51, 109–12; as protestors, 14–15, 53–56, *54, 55,* 61–62. *See also* Free School; public schools and education

Stull, Bradford, 4, 121, 123

Sullivan, Neil: on activities at Free School, 90–91, 93; on educational objectives, 70–74; efforts in preparing Free School, 63–67; on graduation, 118–19; overview of tenure, 61–63; on pedagogy and curriculum, 75–80, 99; on teacher assessments, 96

Swearingen, Jan, 18

team teaching, 78–79

theology, liberation, 45–46, 50, 87

Thurmond, Strom, 32

Tillerson-Brown, Amy, 52

Tirabassi, Katherine, 20

Titus, Jill Ogline, 15, 29, 118

Turner, Kara Miles, 14, 97, 122

ungraded classrooms, 78–79, 88, 98–99, 114

vanden Heuvel, William, 58, 59

Van Jackson, Wallace, 132n5

Virginia Way, 29–30

vocational training, 75, 86, 89–91

The Voice (newsletter), 106, 115, 134n1 (chap. 4)

voter registration drive, 93–94

Walker, Vanessa Siddle, 14, 80

Wall, J. Barrye, 38, 42

Wan, Amy, 4, 11, 120, 125

Ward, Betty, 119

Washington, Booker T., 75

Watkins, Bernetta Stiff, 105, 108–10, 113

Watson, Willie Mae, 65, 73, 80–85, 122

Weaver, Richard M., 133n4

Webster, Noah, 2

white community: allies with Black community, 42–43, 52–53; segregationist rhetoric within, 29–30, 32–37, 38–40; and southern identity, 26–29. *See also* Massive Resistance movement

Whittaker, Katherine, 65

Williams, Heather Andrea, 75

women, as educators, 51–52, 110–11

Woods, Harriet A., 134n3 (chap. 3)

Woodson, James, 31

Woodward, C. Vann, 26

Young, P. B., Sr., 31